Improve People Management And Build Employee Engagement

SADANAND PUJARI

Published by SADANAND PUJARI, 2023.

Also by SADANAND PUJARI

Master The Psychology Of Weight Loss Via Hypnosis Build Healthy Sleep Habits Learn The Art Of Meditation
Improve People Management And Build Employee Engagement

Table of Contents

Copyright

Improve People Management And Build Employee Engagement

Cover design by **SADANAND PUJARI**

Interior design by SADANAND PUJARI

First published in 2023 by

SADANAND PUJARI

About The Book

Welcome to my Book on building employee engagement and improving people management. The Book will help you get the most from your team or work group and give you vital skills to grow as a leader.

Yankelovich and Immerwahr have reported that only 23% of employees say they work at their full potential. Forty-four percent report that they only work hard enough to keep their jobs. And 75% say they could be significantly more effective in their jobs.

And you may be familiar with the Gallup organization which has conducted massive surveys on employee engagement each year since 2000.

Employee engagement is the emotional investment employees make in their organizations. It has to do with passion, motivation, and commitment they bring to their work. Engaged employees care about their work and they care about their team or organization. They want to perform at their best and make a difference to their organizations and the customers they serve.

And, doesn't it stand to reason that those companies who have an engaged and committed workforce are going to outperform those who do not?

The purpose of this Book isn't to teach general theories of leadership but rather to give you specific tools or practices to build a strong team and increase the engagement, motivation, and performance of your employees.

Introduction & Opening Case Study

Hello, friends. Welcome to this incredible Book on cross cultural management. Friends, I will start this Book with the opening case study. The idea is that I want to tell you what really we are trying to achieve in this Book by illustrating this case study, I will give you an idea that how cross-cultural management works in companies, the failure of which can have what kind of impact, the success of which can have, what kind of effects. So those are the things that we will try to understand from this opening case study.

This case study is about the cultural clash between three entities during the merger of these three entities that belonged to the Kalamazoo in Michigan, USA, the parent company and the other two companies that merged with this company in Kalamazoo. The other two being from Stockholm, Sweden and the one from Milan, Italy. Despite being the three entities from the most advanced and industrialized countries, the managers who were involved in the merger of these three entities, they soon realized how much cultural differences existed between these three big entities from such advanced countries.

Culturally they were so different, far apart from each other. I'm talking about a company from Michigan, USA. Kalamazoo. The name of the company is Upjohn Company of USA, which is in the pharmaceutical business that merged with a company in Stockholm, Sweden. The name of that was Pharmacia AB. This merger happened in 1995.

Clash Of Different Management Styles - Case Study Part 2

So, friends, what happened was that there was a clash mainly of the management styles. It started from small, small things like the Swedes generally have their annual vacation in the month of July, and the Italians have their annual vacation for almost the entire month in August. And not knowing this, the managers of Upjohn, Michigan, USA, kept the meetings in the summer months and they found that the employees were not there. The Swedes and the Italians are not available. They are on the beaches. So there were a lot of differences between the people, the employees, as I told you, more than 35,000 employees. Small, small things you know, they are having their own ways of working.

The US company has its own schedules and they say that you are not available. You know, small, small things escalated, actually. So what actually was happening is that the US management style is very traditional in nature. They believe in strong leadership and a command and control style of management that is quite different from the Swedish management style. The aim of that is to build a consensus for any major decisions. So it's not like steep hierarchies that are there in the US system of management. Swedish as well as Italian actually, although there were differences between the Swedish management style and the Italian management style, and there were already clashes among them. But the difference between the European style and the US style played lots of spoilsports.

For example, the Swedish management style was very much informal in nature, who believed in informal meetings and believed in a free working environment that is non intrusive. They never liked an environment with a lot of intrusions from the top and the top-down approach. They did not like the top-down approach of the Michigan company. Swedish management style was founded on the team building, team-based style of working. They believed in taking all their colleagues together and this was their day-to-day style of working. Very importantly, the Swedes believed in the trust. They found it very, very strange that the managers from Michigan, USA, had been always checking on the day to day working.

You know, they were actually constantly monitoring the US as a newly acquired company. They felt that it is their right to ask things and a very strong reporting system was there from the US. So all these things were not really liked by the Swedish employees. Later on, when the US company realized that they have to relax in certain things, they did so, but bad blood was already spilled. So there was a lot of mistrust among the employees and a lot of ill will, disgruntled employees were there from Sweden as well as from Milan, Italy. So that thing had already happened. What had happened, because of these strong differences erupted between the employees from these three different geographical areas. And it really became very difficult to carry on the work smoothly.

Italian Management Style

Now, friends, the Italian style of management was also very distinct, actually. In fact, the takeover of Farmitalia of Italy by Pharmacia AB of Sweden had already created a wedge between the Swedes and the Italians. The Italian style of management is very, very typical. It's quite different in Europe, actually. The worker's status is characterized by the strong distinction between the workers. Because Italians have very, very strong workers unions actually. They are very, very labor specific countries with very, very strong unions and they have a very distinctive status of the workers when compared with the managers. So the Egalitarianism of the Swedes who do not differentiate between the workers and the managers, the single status system of the workers in Sweden strongly clashed with the Italian style of management already.

So the steep hierarchies of the Italian style of management did not gel well with the Swedes already. That problem was already there in Pharmacia. So the Italians, by nature, have a family-first attitude in the working style of the Italians. So sometimes they will leave their job to tend to the children or the family members if somebody is ill or some relative has died. So they will leave jobs and they will go to funerals or any kind of social obligations, they will give first priority to that. And that was absolutely frowned upon by the Swedes. Already these things were happening. So what happened?

The entry of Upjohn actually added to this cultural confusion and the communication problems which were already there between the Swedes and the Italians. That confusion, the barriers to communication, and cultural communication escalated. It has become a very, very strong barrier already.

Impact of Cultural Clashes

So, friends, the overall impact of, you know, this clash of the management styles and the cultural differences, it actually got escalated and the result was a high level of inefficiencies because of the disgruntled employees and, you know, the dominance by the American employees over the Swedish and the Italian employees. Already the friction of culture was there between the Swedes and the Italians. Then the day-to-day monitoring and imposition of the ideas and processes by the American workers led to a lot of delays, making the reports every day.

New reports have to be created on a daily basis. All this led to inefficiencies not only in logistics operations but also in R and D. So basically, the work was added up, the added work of reporting and a lot of canceled meetings because of the distrust and low morale of the Swedes and the Italians. A lot of meetings were getting canceled, which added to the cost. The staff morale was at its lowest which resulted in suboptimal work. The staff was not goal-oriented and they were not performing the way they were supposed to perform. So that added to the cost. And Of course the resistance to work, especially among the Italians as well as the Swedes who were apparently oppressed by the dominance of the American workers, American managers, and their lack of cultural awareness.

Although eventually, they realized. American managers tried to adjust to the management styles of both Swedes as well as the Italians. But it was already too late. The distrust was already there and the employees were disgruntled. And they realized and felt the attitude of the American managers as a direct attack on their way of working. There was a lot of resistance to work, resulting in the departure of some of the key professionals. For example, the head of the R and D department of Pharmacia left. Now, it should be noted that the main reason for the merger of Upjohn with Pharmacia was the marriage between the distribution and supply chain. That is the front end and the back end that is the operations and R and D. R and D were more important because the business of pharmacy depends on the drug pipeline.

The new drugs being launched very often, very frequently of the highest quality, and the order that the R and D department only could bring. And that strength was with Pharmacia, not with Upjohn. At the same time, Pharmacia did not have the front-end strengths that were there with Upjohn. So this marriage of two skills, although both the companies were equals as far as the market capitalization and the position in the market is concerned. But their skills were complementary to each other. And that was the reason for the merger between Upjohn and Pharmacia of Sweden, which had already acquired the Italian Farmitalia. What happened was that the talent from the R and D department leaving had given a great jolt to the very purpose of the very foundation of the merger between U and P?

So this U and P thing did not work because of the talents leaving and that leaving of the talent was the result of the lack of cultural awareness at the very beginning by the American managers. Overall, the delayed product launches took their toll, and by 1997, not only the cost of restructuring increased by US dollar 200 million than what was expected, the total cost came out to be almost close to $1 billion. That is $800 million. So it was a huge cost to U and P and the profits started declining by 1997 and the stock prices of U and P declined by almost 25% on the stock markets. So this was the last nail in the coffin.

I will just explain to you what happened after that and why I am emphasizing on this particular case study to tell you that the lack of cultural awareness can result in awkward outcomes and the failure of the company.

Timelines Of The Events

Let's look at the timelines, all the timelines, and then we'll have a better idea of what actually happened from the very start. So basically, overall, if we say this whole case study talks about the failure to integrate Pharmacia and Upjohn, that the UNP merger did not succeed in the integration, cultural management, and cross-cultural management that is required for the integration. In 1995, after the merger between Upjohn and Pharmacia, that is the new company UNP, along with Italian operations that came to the Pharmacia already in 1993 when they acquired Farmitalia of Italy. So as I have already explained, this merger actually did not go well. They tried their best, but the very lack of cultural awareness and cultural training of the managers managing the 35,000 workforce did not go well. Lack of integration.

Many key persons of the organization left because of mistrust and the failure of the integration and especially the R and D talent. I just told you about it. And it also resulted in cost overruns. By 1997, slow product launches, declining profits, and falling stock prices. So in 1997, because of all these problems, the CEO of UNP actually came from Upjohn before the merger, he was the CEO and in UNP also, he was the CEO. He resigned because he owned the failure of the organization, which was mainly actually the result of the lack of integration, cultural integration. So what happened at that time, the former head of Pharmacia, that person took over this role in order to make things right. Possibly that was the idea. And in 2000, under the leadership of the new CEO, the agricultural domain company, Monsanto, was acquired by UNP. But within one year, the agriculture business was spun off. That was again not a very good decision. The company was now called after the acquisition of Monsanto.

The company was called Pharmacia Corporation. So what has happened now? UNP had become Pharmacia Corporation and the Upjohn name totally vanished, actually. So now there was no Upjohn thing, so it was out of the market. After the 2000 takeover of Monsanto and the spinning off of the Monsanto business in 2001, Monsanto's name had already vanished. I mean, after the merger, after the acquisition. So in 2003, Pharmacia Corporation itself was purchased by Pfizer.

Now that company became Pfizer Inc and Pfizer Inc became the number one pharmaceutical company in the world. The Pharmacia name also vanished. If you look at this timeline, at the very initial stages, the failure of the managers of Upjohn to understand the cultural differences and how to manage them, that very start, that failure got escalated to the extent that within eight years all these names Pharmatalia or Upjohn or Pharmacia or even Monsanto, all names vanished. Things escalated so gravely that ultimately all these things had to be sold off in the market. And ultimately Pfizer had to own all these operations in a single banner. So the result is not only that the Pfizer company became number one in the world, but it is actually bad for the industry also because when many companies become part of a single big company that brings a monopolistic attitude in the industry. A good, healthy industry requires competition.

When all these companies get merged in a single entity, that is not a very good situation for the industry. If there are certain mergers at the local level or even at the international level, but they are scattered. Healthy competition remains in the industry. Because of the failure of the Upjohn managers on the cross cultural management led to one thing after another. And you can see if you look at the timelines, what was the result?

Questions Raised By This Case Study

Now, the idea of this case study Friends was to sensitize you that what we are trying to achieve from this Book, what do we want to learn from this Book? This case study is a very good example. It raises certain questions: what are the things which we have done right and what are the things which we should do right? What skills are required? What is to be done to avoid such kinds of failures, to integrate such kinds of failures to understand the cultural differences and to manage those differences. So some of these questions are not all, but whatever the main questions I have just listed down here in this chapter, these questions will tell you what we want to learn from this Book.

So the first question is related to the kinds of cultural differences that exist when the national cultures from different countries come together to work in a single entity. What kinds of cultural differences are there? So the question is what kind of cultural differences matter when companies from different countries merge with each other? What are the things to look for? What are the areas to look for? So this Book should be able to tell you that.

Now, the second question that comes to the mind of anybody who is a student of cross-cultural management books is to understand the ways to understand the different national cultures. So how to map the world, how to understand the differences between two countries, how to compare. Is there any tool available, an easy tool, maybe through the internet, or through some online resources? Can we compare and understand the cultures of the world? That's very interesting. That's very important. If you can understand the culture if you are already aware these differences are there, and if those differences are there, what to do and what does it mean Actually, if the differences are there, so does the case study indicates a match between the described characteristics and what we know from our knowledge about this understanding of the different national cultures. So, for example, the differences between different aspects of culture, different dimensions of culture between Italian workers, Swedish workers, and American workers, do we know these things?

Do we know these differences? Do we know the differences of the management style? And if the management style differences are there, how are they going to impact the overall results? So are we aware of these things? In fact, in this case study, that was a very major failure. It will be very, very clear at the end of this Book. Now, the third question relates to cross-cultural management. So these differences, we know that these are the differences. But what to do with these differences? So should we not do any mergers, any international mergers? Because the differences exist, because the types of things that happen to UNP would again happen or can it be avoided? So what could have been done right by the managers in this case study? So we should be able to tell after doing this Book what went wrong and what could have been done right. To become capable of doing that this Book is required. Then the issue related to the imposition of somebody's own culture, the ethnocentric approach of the company who acquires another company internationally. So why does the parent company want to impose its ways on the acquired company?

Why do they do that? Why does it happen? What is human psychology in that? Or organizational psychology or organizational behavior. Why do companies think that way? What is failure? Why is this probably a failure of the companies in imposing their own cultural ethnocentric approach that actually results in the fiascos of the type which happened with UNP? Why do the companies do that? Are they not trained in that, how to manage those differences? And then cultural awareness, the dimension of cultural awareness that what level and kind of cultural awareness is required. We know the national differences, but are we aware of how to live with those cultural differences?

Do we have that kind of awareness? Is the awareness of the cultural differences that exist across the organization, across all the managers at different levels? What kind of penetration of the awareness is required? And the very, very important question that is the mother of all the questions. Can the local ways, local management styles be left to their own stage and not impose the ways of the parent company at all. Leave it to the local silos. Do we leave the local ways of doing things and trust that the results will be as desired by the parent company? So can the local units be left to use their own ways of doing things and still achieve the results? That's a $1 million question.

I will not be telling you the answers to these questions right now. What I want is for you to do this very concise and quick Book on cross-cultural management that will go into the related topics that relate to these questions and we will try to understand the different researches, different ideas and different tips and techniques for doing this kind of cross-cultural management and avoid such situations. That is the main aim of this Book.

Impact Of Globalization

So friends, in this case study what we have tried to understand . In fact, this case study proves that going global is not an easy task. So it's not a usual kind of merger or market entry or whatever, any kind of interaction, overseas interaction, business interaction, any kind of transaction, an international transaction is not an easy task actually, because of the differences. People are different, nations are different. So sheer lack of awareness of cross-cultural differences, as this case study has very clearly indicated, can lead to major failures of the type that I just explained in this particular case study. And it can definitely impact very severely on the bottom lines of the company.

To the extent that the brand, the company may vanish from the market. And that is exactly what happened with UNP in this case study. This case study will become a basis for us to understand the concepts of cross-cultural management in this Book. So we'll take it forward from there. First things first, in order to understand the importance of cross-cultural management, it should be noted that the number of people working for overseas companies around the world has already crossed 100,000,000 in 2021 and it is increasing and why it is increasing, why the involvement of the people is there with the overseas companies. That is the impact of globalization for better opportunities, better salaries, and a better working environment. People choose between domestic companies as well as overseas companies. If you, for example, take the example of the Indian market, there are Indian companies, there are foreign companies.

The first choice of any person in India to work with is a foreign company, irrespective of the number of working hours or whatever it is. In totality the whole package is better with overseas companies. This is a general view in India. Most of the fresh graduates, most of the talented people, first give interviews for the foreign companies, especially from North America or from Western Europe and sometimes Japan also. With this first choice being the overseas companies. It is obvious that the number of people working in overseas companies is increasing exponentially. And because of this globalization, the companies also find it very suitable, useful, and economically viable to have overseas operations. So what is the result of this? That we have a kind of multicultural workforce environment in these companies. So it has become the norm.

Multicultural workforce has become the norm. And as I will tell you in this Book later, there are certain theories that say that the performance of the multicultural workforce is better than the monoculture groups, monoculture workforce. These things are all debatable and a lot of research is being done. Your deeper study on diversity management and multicultural workforce management will be really useful. Multicultural workforce management requires understanding and adapting to these cultural differences. First of all, what are the differences? Secondly, how the process of adaptation happens. But adapting is required. Understanding is required.

What Is Culture?

So, friends, what exactly is culture? This is the first question that comes to our mind. Let me tell you, there are many definitions of culture and probably you already know what culture is. You already have read this topic on culture. In some Books, you already are aware of what is culture, but we will try to understand the culture from the point of view of managing the multicultural workforce and managing mergers, international mergers, acquisitions, or any kind of business activity that we do beyond national borders. So the unique preferences, beliefs, and values in a very, very short description, you can say that the culture comprises these unique preferences, beliefs, and values, or it can be also said as the collective programming of the mind in a particular work environment or society. So collective programming. Why?

Because the cultural elements are many hundreds of cultural elements are there. The sum total of many cultural elements like beliefs, societal rules, lifestyles, techniques, institutions, religion, ethnicity, artifact, and numerous other cultural factors like societal rules, the hierarchies. There are so many things in society that shape the social fabric of the people on how it should work and how it is behaving, how it actually works. So that shape is defined by several elements. So that makes the cultural understanding and the understanding of the culture more complex, more complicated.

Complexity Of Understanding Cultural Differences

So let us see whether we can do something about understanding the cultures because it is not possible for business persons to know all the cultures of the world. It's not possible because every culture is unique. Like you have different faces in the world. It is very, very rare that you can find two people with the same looks. You will be able to differentiate between the face of one person with another. So that diversity is there in the facial expression. The same type of diversity exists in the cultures. Within the countries also, there can be different cultures, but there has to be some way for business people to categorize things, to make it simple, to understand cultures and should be able to categorize in such a way that they can take international business decisions, they can manage multicultural workforces, can smoothly integrate any mergers or acquisitions or smoothly carry out international trade.

For example, if we talk of the culture of one Country, USA, they may have cultural element one, cultural element two, cultural element three, cultural element four, five and so on. Similarly, the culture of Japan will have many, many cultural elements. Similarly, the culture of Germany. We may have many, many elements. So hundreds of elements, Chinese culture, hundreds of elements. Indian culture will have its own set of cultural elements: religion, society, societal fabric, societal rules, institutions, infrastructure, working style, and management style. So many cultural elements are there the basis of these cultural elements it is next to impossible for a business person to understand the culture. It is not possible.

My idea was to tell you that it is really, really, really complicated to understand the culture in its raw form. The cultural complexity is further increased by what the behavior of the individual and his interpersonal relationship with his or her colleagues or with society or the external environment, and Of course, institution and organization and the community, the relationships and communication between organizations and institutions in the community and the structures and systems of the nations, countries. So the federal, state, and local regulations, and laws built-in the environment of things like public works, infrastructure, and what kind of ecosystem exists around an individual, make this understanding of this culture very, very complex. I will give you an example.

In the same country, in the same city, there are regions and parts of the city that are of a different economic strata. Demography is different and in another part, the demography is different for a number of reasons. Infrastructure is one of those. Infrastructure and the types of people who have settled in a particular part of the city. You will find that the behavior of the people in the same city, in the same country may be different. They are different. They will behave differently. And this fact we understand, everybody knows it. Who has been in any urban area anywhere in the world. They know that within the city you have different blocks and parts of the city and the regions in the city that behave differently because of many reasons. But the infrastructure and the environment play an important role. That was just one idea. That was just one example I gave you to make you understand that the cultural complexity in its raw form is really very, very intense, unmanageable. So for business people, it doesn't work actually, business people cannot really understand the culture in its raw form. It's not possible.

Summary

So, friends, we just talked about globalization and its impact on the importance of understanding and managing the cultural differences across the work teams with different cultural backgrounds. Let us look at the summary of the things that we have learned in this module on globalization and cultural differences. What we now understand from this module is that globalization has changed the composition of the workplaces, or we can say the profile of the workplaces around the world in terms of the cultural differences. So we have more and more multicultural teams and now we even have remote teams.

We have work from the home culture that is gaining momentum and we have highly multicultural work teams in place. It is all because of the globalization and increasing importance of global trade. More and more people are now working with foreign companies either in their own country or they are working abroad. The preferences of most people, especially from developing countries, are for the foreign companies. I gave you an example of India. In India, there is a definite preference for foreign companies to work. There has been an increased migration of skilled as well as non-skilled workforce. The flow of which has increased in the last few decades.

The most advanced and rich countries are seeing an inflow of foreign workers, both skilled and unskilled. This situation has led to an increasing importance of understanding cultural differences, and understanding of the ways to manage intercultural work teams at multicultural workplaces. In this module, we also learned that culture itself is a very, very complex concept of study. It has to be understood from several perspectives, and this complexity of understanding culture increases with an infinite set of factors attached to the dynamically changing macro and micro environment around the local cultures. So much preserved local cultures, despite all the modernism and materialism that we see today. In the facade of this materialism lies underneath the traditional cultures and the will of the local people to preserve the local ways of the yesteryears.

Finally, the individuals themselves have their traits, and that itself makes understanding of the culture very, very complex. We also learned in this module that it is a piece of good news, that it is possible to understand world cultures and cultural differences to the extent that it can help in carrying out international trade, international business and to be able to take strategic international business decisions. So that's a very comforting situation. It is very much possible, despite the complexity of the culture that we have seen in this Book. Going forward in the Book, we will see how we can carry out this kind of understanding and use the different cultural models and tools to be able to manage cross-cultural teams and to increase cross-cultural competency. These were the main points that we gathered that are the takeaways from this module. If you think that there are any more takeaways that I might have missed, do share in the Q and A chapter of this Book.

Culture And Human Behavior

Friends. Do you know that the study of culture and human behavior, attitudes, beliefs, and norms require a group of following types of experts. A variety of experts are required who are expected to work in tandem to get the understanding and results that can be used to understand a culture that is so complex. People like psychologists, social scientists, anthropologists, demographers, historians and field research specialists are the most common type of experts that we require to work on projects, research projects to carry out long research on understanding the cultures, because culture can only be understood through surveys and field study.

Globe Implicit Leadership Research study was a ten-year-long, survey-based research study that was started in 2004. So it was such a long study for these very popular research studies that have been helping the industry very much. They really took a lot of time. More than 200 researchers from almost 62 countries studied almost 100,000 respondents to carry out this very, very large research that we will be talking about in this module. Geert Hofstede, who is a Dutch social scientist, developed his original model as a result of using the Factor analysis to examine the cultural study results of a worldwide survey of the employees of IBM started from 1967 until 1973, and many of his new dimensions came later. Such long studies were involved in getting these insights and results of cultural differences, understanding of the cultural differences.

Low and High Context Cultures Model

So what is required? Friends: How is it done in business? They look for the models, cultural models because that is easy to understand. They can find some differences, some way of categorizing the world cultures, and national cultures, using these cultural models. There are hundreds of models available in the market, but the most popular models are practically used in business I am going to discuss. So to start with, I will take up the very popular but very simple model that describes world cultures and national cultures in the context of the context, which means they are either low-context or low context cultures or high or higher context cultures.

What do they display? There is a continuum that describes a particular culture. Where does it exist on this continuum? Whether it is the very low context culture or moderately low context culture or moderately high context culture or neutral culture. It can be neutral culture or it can be high context culture. This is one of the simplest models that works like a thumb rule for cross-cultural management, for the understanding of world culture. Higher the lower context of the culture it signifies that the communication done by the people belonging to those cultures will be more specific, more detailed and more precise. This model is based on the observation, experience of the business people, and they indicate weaknesses in terms of the ability to decode unspoken messages. They find it very, very difficult to understand body language because they are more like black and white. So communication for them is verbal.

What do you say? They will like to believe it. You say yes, but the body language says no. They will take it as yes. No no, they will not have any doubts. They will say it is yes only because you said yes. But your body language, and your facial expression is saying something else. So they have this weakness. In A lower context this weakness will be more for body language. So unspoken messages and body language, they find it very, very difficult. One very good example is of the business people who go to Japan. That is a very high context culture. Japanese culture, where they communicate more by body language, and unspoken words, than verbal communication, specific communication or detailed communication. Definitely not. High context culture and it is very, very distinct, Japanese culture. So what happens is that the business people find it really difficult to deal with Japan when it comes to business. So it becomes very challenging despite Japan being a very, very lucrative market, most of the foreigners find it very, very difficult to exploit the Japanese market. Higher the context of the culture, the communication is less direct.

Emphasis is on human relations. For example, in Japan there are things like keiretsu. So what is keiretsu? Keiretsu are business networks, business clusters, business groupings, relationships, business relationships of the local people in such a way that they will give first preference for doing any backward integration or backward purchases or any kind of financial or business dealings within the group, within the keiretsu. To an extent, in certain cases in such groups, they will have a financial stake in each other's companies also. So their business depends on human relations or organization relations, and it is less direct. So why do they do it, you will never understand. How does it help? It is by experience. So there is no theory behind it. They will not be able to explain why they do it like this. That is Japanese culture. So they believe in human relations. More sensitive. They are more sensitive, and very strong in these non-verbal things.

For example, I'm taking again the example of Japan only that when you work in Japan, you have to understand the air. That is what they say. It's a very common saying in the local area that you have to understand the air. You need not believe in your ears or you need not look for the spoken words from the Japanese, even if they are your employees, even if they are your well-wishers, they will not be able to tell you or really what is to be done. So you have to read the air. So they are very, very sensitive to nonverbal gestures and communication and the feelings of others. So even within the business, they will try to read the air and your feeling and their feeling and whether you are on the right track. And if you are not on the right track, things are going to go haywire. So when we talked of the case study of UNP, where the organizations involved were from North America, Sweden and Italian regions, it was still manageable, and much simpler to manage, which actually UNP could not do. But it was not difficult because, after all, they are Western countries.

After all, they have certain historical connections. But if one of the entities would have been from Japan in this particular case study, the situation would have been even worse, actually. And if some Japanese company had been acquired by an American company, that is what exactly happened when Vodafone acquired the third-largest telecom company in Japan. It is a J-phone. So I will give you that case study. I will share with you a case study of the acquisition of the J-phone in the Japanese market by Vodafone for almost more than $20 billion. And something similar happened as happened in the case of the UNP. So that case study I will include in this Book later, this low context culture and high context culture plays a very, very important role. It has to be understood.

Failure of Vodafone in Japan - A Case Study of High Context Culture

So, friends, as I just mentioned to you, let us take one small case study about investment in Japan. One of the major opportunities in Japan is the mergers and acquisitions that are happening. And that's a big opportunity which is there now. The government of Japan is also open to many industries for M and A, in spite of the fact that the big chunk of the mergers and acquisitions that are happening at this stage at this time in Japan are among the local competitors itself, local companies itself. But still there exists a lot of scope, a lot of gap and a lot of possibilities for foreign investments. Vodafone acquired J-phone somewhere in early 2000, and this j-phone was Japan's third-largest telecom operator, and the value of the transaction was almost $20 billion.

It was a very big ticket investment by Vodafone and a 100% stake was there. So it was fully acquired by Vodafone. J-phone was the first company in Japan to introduce a camera phone, So that was a very major innovation of J-phone, which was a very big success factor, actually. But Vodafone actually failed in Japan after years of making mistakes and wasting time not understanding the market, making several assumptions about the Japanese market and the local people, and the local recruited persons, making a lot of assumptions and failing to do the preparation and understand the Japanese customer. Vodafone failed in Japan and finally sold the Japan Telecom-J-phone-Vodafone KK combine to SoftBank at a much lower price and with a lot of losses. Now we have to look at the most interesting part of this story, and that is the facts.

The fact is that the Vodafone failure had nothing to do with the closed nature of the Japanese government, which is generally alleged. Most foreign companies, when they fail in Japan, blame the Japanese government. So case to case, it has to be understood what is the role of the closed nature of the Japanese government in the failure of the different companies and their involvement in Japanese business? But as far as the Vodafone case is concerned, it had nothing to do with the closed nature of the Japanese government. So it was not there. And the fact that SoftBank turned around the company within six months after acquiring it. So it is not that SoftBank had any special consideration for the Japanese government or it was planned like this.

Nothing, nothing of that sort. It was purely commercial decision-making where Vodafone failed. So I will just tell you about the two main reasons why Vodafone failed in Japan. And you can read a lot of research papers on this topic, and a lot of analysis you can read. Most of these research papers and analysis boils down to two main reasons why Vodafone failed. And those two reasons come from the lack of preparation, making a lot of assumptions by Vodafone and not really understanding the Japanese market. So what went wrong? The two reasons were the first reason was Vodafone's failure to make further investments and where? Further investment in creating a much larger mobile network infrastructure. So that was the failure.

What was required was big coverage, a lot of new investment in new equipment and technology that Vodafone did not do, probably because they already had invested $20 billion and they never had the possibility of further investment. And that is again the failure of the planning that you are paying handsomely to acquire a company. And it may be an impulsive decision. I really do not know the facts of the case, but whatever it is that after spending $20 billion, there was no scope for Vodafone to do this very, very important and very critical investment in the network infrastructure. And the second failure of Vodafone was the failure to offer mobile handsets, as expected by the Japanese customers who are very, very demanding. J-phone was known for introducing the camera phone in the mind of the Japanese customer since Vodafone acquired the J-phone. They will introduce even better features and it was possible for

Vodafone to observe and read the air and understand what type of new mobile handsets are required to be offered to the Japanese customer in light of the competitors. And what is happening with the other two major operators. It was possible. So that was the failure and what SoftBank did. SoftBank realized this very fast. And these are the two things. These were the two gaps where SoftBank invested the money and offered the right type of mobile handset, and within six months the company turned around. So it was a very major success story of SoftBank, a very successful transaction of SoftBank. The question is what actually went wrong behind the scenes? How is it possible for a company like Vodafone that is a multinational company and that has the best of the talent management talent, knowing the world, having worked in various countries, what actually happened in Japan? What made it difficult for Vodafone to understand and pinpoint?

Understand the very simple things like these two things, the network infrastructure requirement and the judgment about the expectations of the Japanese customer that was so easily done by SoftBank, a company that is based in Japan itself. So they know Japanese culture. They know Japanese people. In my understanding, as per my research, Vodafone's main failure was that they did not realize that they are dealing with a culture that is high context culture, high context culture, which means they are very sensitive to nonverbal communication and body language. So they do not speak out very precisely, with very detailed answers to the questions. So the type of culture that Vodafone was dealing with for so long was normally low context culture, and the extent of high context that existed in Japan resulted in the failure of Vodafone to integrate Vodafone with J-phone so that the local employees could not guide Vodafone on the first issue and secondly, also on understanding the Japanese customer and rather Vodafone, even if they would have done some surveys of the Western type market surveys of the western type, they failed to realize that the customer in the surveys would not divulge whatever they are thinking, whatever they are liking, whatever their preferences.

What is required is to understand from the air, from the market, by body language, and by the nonverbal, including the written communication. It is a very, very clear case of the failure of Vodafone to understand the high-context culture and failure in the integration and failure in the understanding of customer preferences because of the very distinct and peculiar culture that Japan is.

Hofstede's Model Of National Cultural Dimensions

Now, friends, let us talk about the very popular cultural model, the second most popular cultural model that is a little more complicated than the low-context, high-context culture model. This model is extremely popular despite being a little more complicated. It was suggested by a Dutch scientist, social scientist Geert Hofstede, and it is called the Geert Hofstede Cultural Dimensions Model. So what Geert Hofstede did was that instead of categorizing the world cultures based on the low context or high context or based on cultural elements, that was next to impossible. What he did he listed out certain dimensions of the culture, certain characteristics of the culture, certain features of the culture that were relevant to the businesses, the people who are into mergers and acquisition, people who are into international business, the things that meant for the business, decisions for the market entry decisions for any kind of international operations decisions. So according to him, as per his research, the first very important dimension was the power distance that indicates either the low score or the high score.

High score means that the people with the culture having the high power distance score embraces hierarchy, while the cultures, which means national cultures, which means countries with low power distance score embraces egalitarianism. So I will tell you a little more detail about this dimension in my next chapter. And then the second dimension that was identified by Hofstede is called collectivism versus individualism. And the high score in this particular dimension indicates a culture that is described as the individualistic culture, while the cultures with low scores are described as collective cultures collectivist culture. So, for example, Japan has a very low score, a reasonably low score, less than the average score in this. So it is very much collective. When we compared with many other cultures.

Similarly, if we talk of the third dimension that was identified by Geert Hofstede, it is called UAI in short, which means Uncertainty awareness index and a high score in UAI indicates the discomfort of the people in the culture with the awkward results of any work which they do, any uncertainty involved in any kind of actions that they carry out, any business activity they carry out, they feel very, very uncomfortable with being not able to actually face the awkward results of any project or program that they are carrying out. So they will do a lot of planning. They will spend a lot of time in pre-planning and making and organizing the activities, which is to be carried out to avoid any wrong results or awkward results. So less risk taking. And the cultures that show a low score on the Uncertainty Awareness index are very much comfortable with uncertainty and they are risk takers. They are ready to face any bad results or failures. They treat the failures as the future success.

The fourth dimension that was identified by Geert Hofstede was femininity versus masculinity. The high score on this particular dimension indicates that the cultures of these countries with these high scores recognize the importance of the power of the people, the masculine characteristics that are there as against the feminist characteristics that are displayed by the cultures, national cultures with a low score on this particular dimension, where the importance is given to nurturing workers, the workplace environment, organization, very, very feminist kinds of characteristics. So I will tell you more details about it in later chapters. The fifth dimension is called the short-term versus long-term orientation. Very clearly. Very obviously indicating the high score in certain cultures, indicating the futuristics and long-term planning. Having the fore vision for a very good future of the organization, of the product line, of the country, of the society. Certain societies have a very, very long-term view as well as long-term planning. And the low score in this particular dimension indicates the traditional nature of the societies thinking very, very short term.

The slaves of the tradition, slaves of the rituals, and the slaves of historical thinking, old school of thoughts. So those kinds of societies indicate low scores on this particular dimension. And last but not the least, the cultural dimension is called restraint versus indulgence which indicates that a high score in indulgence indicates the importance is given to the entire satisfaction that is supposed to be good. So indulgence is supposed to be good. But on the other hand, a low score on this dimension indicates normative repression, restraints. These were the dimensions that were identified by Geert Hofstede. A lot of research was done. More than 50,000 companies employees he used for this survey and online he is still doing these surveys for many, many years.

And the online data, the latest data is easily available on the Internet, free of cost. So you can find the scores of different countries on these dimensions. And if you understand all these dimensions fully, you will understand and will be able to compare two different cultures on these very limited cultural dimensions. Instead of going into an infinite number of cultural elements. So that is the advantage of this particular model.

Hofstede's Model Of National Cultural Dimensions Explained - Part 1

So friends. Power distance Index indicates that the cultures with high power distance scores, tend to accept the existence of the most powerful people in society and their position and their right to rule the masses. And they accept the hierarchy. They accept their seniority. For example, the score of Japan in this power distance is quite high and you see a lot of hierarchy in Japan. So I will show you in my next few chapters, I will show you the scores of several countries on this particular dimension as well as on the other dimensions. And then we will talk about it.

What it means is that the power distance, high power distance indicates the acceptance of society, of the acceptance of privileges that are enjoyed by certain powerful people in society. I just want to tell you that this power distance index does indicate some important aspects of the people management in the business and the organization in a multicultural environment. So there are certain cultures that tend to accept the authority of the people and there are certain cultures with a low score on the power index will definitely indicate the lack of acceptance of the authoritarian way of working in particular countries.

So these things have a lot of importance for the businesses, for the international operations. So if we talk in a little more detail about the popular cultural model, number two, in terms of the individualism versus collectivism dimension of the culture of the Hofstede, we find that the societies which indicate that individualistic characteristics have a high score on individualism and the societies and the cultures with low score indicate the collectivism. So what happens when the way of working changes drastically?

The management styles of the countries change very, very drastically in the individualistic societies and the collective societies. So you will find the differences very, very stark. In my next chapter, I will give you a comparison between the management styles of the Japanese businesses and the management styles of the US businesses. So you will have an understanding that individualistic societies have very, very starkly different management styles versus the management styles of the collectivist society. So this thing will be more clear to you in the next chapter in my example, which I will be giving. So the traits of the individualistic cultures, is the self-sufficiency, uniqueness of themselves being unique or their work being unique, and the independence of work, freedom to work.

So for example, if you take the example of the US, the US has a very high score on the individualism dimensions of the Geert Hofstede model. There is a lot of focus on individual freedom of work in US companies and Of course autonomy. So, these are the traits of individualistic societies which are quite different in the case of collectivist societies, where some of the features include rewards and compensation for the team, appreciation for the team rather than the individuals, which is very quite different from the individualistic societies. Uncertainty avoidance of the Hofstede cultural model indicates the propensity of societies to avoid any kind of uncertain results. Awkward results. So one of the most uncertain avoidance cultures in the world is Japan. So I will just show you the scores of many of these countries. We will have a comparison also of the countries you will get to know the comparison.

We will do the comparisons. Then you will understand. So Japan is one of the most uncertainty-avoidance countries where the people are very much less risk taker. In a society with a high score on Uncertainty avoidance, there is a low tolerance, they worry about the future. They are more loyal to their employers. They accept seniority on the basis of leadership and position. High tolerance of uncertainty avoidance, which means the low scores on uncertainty avoidance indicate that the particular society welcomes risk taking. They welcome the change. They even welcome the rule change if it is good for the organization.

Uncertainty avoidance is a very, very important dimension, and definitely when we go further and when we do the comparison, you will have a better idea of the comparisons among the countries. How does it work?

Hofstede's Model Of National Cultural Dimensions Explained - Part 2

Hello, friends. So do you agree that people behave very differently in terms of gender? There are visible differences in the ways of the females and the males and what kinds of traits they show. You can easily observe these differences. If you can observe these differences between the male traits and the female traits, you might have realized when you meet people internationally, did you ever see that the people of a particular country or a particular ethnicity, people of a particular region, are more behaving like female traits, whether they are male or female, but their way of working is more feminine in nature.

You must have noticed this thing. Very rightly, Also realized that the cultures of the world display masculine or feminine traits. There is a continuum. Some cultures are highly masculine. Some cultures are highly feminine cultures. So what are the traits that differentiate these cultures? When we say that they are more masculine in the ways of doing things and it is more feminine in ways of doing things? So typically speaking, the opinion of people from a masculine culture is that man's role is to rule and woman's role is to raise the children. Now again, it depends on the level of masculinity. So how much more masculine a country is, then you will find that this opinion is stronger.

At a national cultural level, it is easy to find out what they think about a particular aspect. Scientists like Geert Hofstede actually used a very elaborate questionnaire to find out these opinions, and he differentiated the different cultures of the world on these aspects. And another thing that typically opines people from a masculine culture is that the gender differences exist, which means gender roles are distinct, explicit, and concrete. So that's again a masculine trait. And Of course, in extreme cases, masculine cultures indicate that men should dominate in society. Do you also think that men should dominate in a society? So think about it and think about your own culture. What the majority of people say when you compare with other countries and other cultures, is it that your people, people around you, the people of your country, your colleagues, your friends, do they think more in terms of the conviction that men should dominate in society? So think about it. And independence is the highest ideal. So being independent generally the male trait is not dependent on others. So think about it.

Think about your culture, the people around you, and the culture of your country. And if you can really find out the differences by the end of this particular module, you will already know how you can compare your traits with other countries. It's not difficult. Now, further, in the masculine culture, people who achieve success are worthy of admiration. This is generally the belief. So success matters in such kinds of cultures. So I'll give you an example. It is easy to find out whether it is true in your culture. So look at the brand ambassadors, look at the advertisements of certain things, and look at the profile of these influencers who are used in these kinds of advertisements.

So for example, I take the example of India. So in India, if there is some particular new product that has been launched in the market by a big company, they will use somebody like Amitabh Bachchan because he is a very famous actor. He has been highly successful in his life, even at the age of more than 75, he is still earning huge money. He is a rich person, he is a powerful person. He is a very famous person. And that person can bring business to a particular brand in an advertisement. So that will work in India because Indian opinion is more towards highly successful people. So that's masculine trait is there in India. So look at your own country, look at your own people, and very importantly, look at the advertisements

What kinds of personalities, and influencers are used in your country, in your advertisements, and you will know whether your culture is more attracted towards success or something else. I will tell you something else. But that is something that can be done by you. And there is a general observation in a masculine culture that ambitions lead to action. Such an ambitious person. He has got a lot of ambition. It's not that the feminine culture does not have ambition, but the level of ambition of achieving great heights is actually more in masculine cultures. And the general belief is that without these ambitions, people will not act, People will become lazy, so people will work hard if there are ambitions, masculine ambitions. So that is the thing which you should check.

Can you tell me about your culture and your people? What do they think about it? So find it out. In the masculine culture, highly masculine culture the general saying is that the great and the fast are beautiful. So look at the Hollywood movies. Very gigantic movies, huge budget movies, fast-running movies. So look at the plot of such movies, which works very well in the US and many of the countries in the world, Hollywood movies. So you will get an idea which are the places where what kind of movies are liked, and you will get a picture of the culture of the different countries. Finally but that is not the only thing, there are many other things when we talk about the masculine culture, such as the belief that you live to work. So work becomes your religion in a masculine culture. As opposed to these things, when we talk of a more feminine culture, the typical opinion of people from a feminine culture is that men are also involved in children's upbringing.

So there is a kind of equality that is required, that is that culture is not gender biased and the roles are not gender specific. So if the woman is supposed to take care of the children, it is the duty of the man also. So they have to switch roles every now and then in such kinds of cultures. And Of course, the gender roles are not explicit and concrete and not fixed actually. Gender roles are interchangeable. Look at your culture. What do you think? What do you feel? Are gender roles interchangeable in your society, in your culture? Compare it with other cultures and you will find the differences. The differences do exist. If you talk of, for example, the countries like Afghanistan or other countries of the Islamic world, you will find that generally, the gender roles are not interchangeable, they are more masculine culture and this factor is reflected in the Hofstede model and in this Book I will take some examples and you will know better.

I will show you these things in more detail in my subsequent chapters where I will be comparing the scores on different dimensions, including masculinity and femininity for at least four different countries. And later on, I'll give you a very detailed comparison between the Japanese and the US culture using Hofstede's scores. And in the feminine culture, the general opinion of the people is that the genders should be treated equally as against the opinion of the masculine societies, that men should dominate the society. And in the feminine cultures, the cultures indicate more feminine traits, mutual dependence is the main ideal against the masculine culture where independence is the highest ideal. This difference is also very much visible. Then in the feminine culture, the people who handle adversity deserve appreciation and they are liked. So as against the people who achieve success are worthy of admiration in the masculine culture, people who do good for society, who face adversity, and who fight all the odds to get success for not only themselves but for the society.

They are the most admired people and you will see this in their country ads, country-specific ads, business ads on TV or in the newspapers you will find the influencers and the brand ambassadors are not very, very successful and rich people, but the people who are in the news for doing some good service for society, for coming out of adversity in their life or in their work or in social work. So that's a very major difference, you will find. For example, if you look at the countries from Scandinavia, countries like Sweden, Finland, and Denmark, you will find this kind of trait very much because they are very feminine types of cultures. Then the opinion of the masculine cultures is that ambition leads to action.

In the case of feminine culture, the general saying is that service is the greatest motivator to action. So people work for providing services, for helping others, for contributing to society, achieving something for the benefit of all for the greater good. So that difference is very much there. And then the little and the slow are beautiful as against the masculine culture which says that the great and the fast are beautiful. So you will find the most popular movies and the plots for the theatrical items in the feminine cultures that will indicate the slow-moving movies, very romantic, and very soft movies you will find as against the many of the big budget Hollywood movies.

You will find those differences. And as against the masculine cultures that generally adhered to the slogan that you live to work. The slogan of the people of a feminine culture is more towards your work to live. You earn money for a better life. You don't work for money, but you work for living a good, enjoyable, and relaxed life. So these differences exist. So whatever I have said, whatever I have discussed with you, do you really think that those differences exist? Can you appreciate the fact that the differences are there? So please look at your own culture and if you want to comment on the Q n A chapter or any direct messaging on this Book, you can do that. So what is your opinion about this? I would be very, very happy to know.So when you give your opinion, you should mention which country you belong to.

Hofstede's Model Of National Cultural Dimensions Explained - Part 3

Now, friends, just think about it. Do you think that there is something where you differentiate one person from another person on the fore vision, long term thinking, short term thinking? Do you see those differences around you? If you see those differences around you, the existence of such differences among people in our society also means that among the national cultures on the global scale, the same differences, you will find people of one particular culture with another culture. So it is also very interesting to note that the type of differences that we see around may not be with very big gaps within the cultures, but on an international level, when you compare the cultures of different countries, you also find similar differences on a very broader scale. So that is what actually Geert Hofstede got. And those differences that matter to the businesses, that matter to international trading operations, those slowly and steadily he captured. In the same line he also picked up this cultural dimension in the popular model that is model number two that I am referring to, and that is long-term thinking versus short-term thinking.

So according to Geert Hofstede, there are national cultures that are very short-term thinking, national cultures. Short-term thinking means they adhere more to the rituals and the old thinking, and they don't really want to, they don't want to innovate or invest in the future of society. So such societies will not think for the long term benefit. They will be looking for short term benefits. Generally, these societies tend to get triggered by small problems. So you might have heard about the riots which happened in, for example, in the USA- Capitol Hill riots. You know, about. Now US society is proven to be a short-term thinking society and with the little instigation by a head of state, the population of the USA even went for the riots and to the apex political building of the country.

The thinking is so short-term, but there are countries like Japan. There are countries like China. There are many European countries that think long term. Germany is another country that has a culture of thinking long-term, and there you will not find people who would be instigated with small cues or small triggers. It will not happen in those countries or those cultures. So those differences exist and short-term thinking and long-term thinking have a lot of implications, business implications. This dimension has been a really very important dimension. I will talk a little bit more about it when I take the example of the comparison of certain countries in the next few chapters. Then we will talk about it more.

What do you think? Do you feel that there would be differences in the societies, in the world, national cultures of these kinds of differences, short term thinking and long term? Think of a country like Pakistan that at one time had a short-term Hofstede's score of almost near to zero, such a low score on Hofstede. And in fact, at one time it was the lowest in the world. What do you think? Do you agree that such differences exist among the cultures of the world with respect to long term thinking and short term thinking? Just think about it. And if you want to comment, you can comment.

Another very, very important cultural dimension of the Geert Hofstede model is restraint versus indulgence. So as the name suggests, restraint means there are certain cultures in the world comparatively, they tend to restrain themselves with bodily comforts or the approach is not towards enjoying life. It is more towards work, workaholism it is called. For example, if you take the example of Japan that is having a very low score in indulgence, are very workaholics, they are loners. They generally will not enjoy the money that they have. They are already cash rich. Their accounts are full of cash. Still, they will not enjoy that money. And that money keeps on piling in their accounts.

This is a very interesting example of Japan which has a very low score in indulgence. So we will talk about it more later. There are countries like the USA that have extremely high scores when it comes to indulgence. So they have the society even if they don't have money, they will like to indulge, what will they do? Can you tell me? They will use their credit cards? The US is the country. If, when, if there is no money in the pocket or in the bank account, if they have credit cards, they will go for something indulging, some hobbies which they cannot avoid. They will go hiking. Money is not a barrier for many of the people in these cultures like in the US. So they will borrow money, but they will indulge in worldly pleasures.

What do you think? Do you feel that such differences exist between the countries? But let me tell you a very important thing, it is possible that within a society also there may be differences among the people. Some people are more indulgent, some people are more restrained within their societies. But what happens from the business angel, individual cultural differences do not really make any benefit to the business. So businesses take decisions, market entry decisions, acquisition decisions, merger decisions or alliance decisions internationally in such a way that they reflect broader and cumulative differences. So when we say that the majority of the people in the US are adhering to indulgence, it means the culture of the US from a business point of view is more indulgent than Japanese culture. So that's very important and that should be in your mind. So on that note, you should check the difference between your own culture and the cultures of the other countries. So if you feel you think that your culture is more indulgent or less indulgent, write it down. Write the comments, but let me know the country of your origin.

Cultural Dimensions Wise Country Scores Analysis With Examples Of 4

So now, friends, let us try to apply this knowledge of the Power Distance Index. Individualism versus collectivism Index. Masculinity versus Femininity Index. Uncertainty Avoidance Index. Long term versus short term index. And restraint versus. Indulgence. So on these dimensions, let us compare countries. First is Brazil. Number two is China. Number three is Germany, and number four is USA. You can include another set of countries in this kind of example, which I'm taking. What you can do, you can include your country also, and you make this chart and then you will be able to understand where your culture stands. So this is a very good exercise for you.

Just look at this example that I am discussing. Look at the diagram which I'm showing and create the same diagram. Whether you use your Excel sheet or whatever tool you use, make your diagram with all these four countries and write down the scores of Hofstede for your country and write an analysis about your culture when you compare with other countries. So I will show you and I will demonstrate to you how you analyze this kind of data. So I will explain this to you. Let me tell you this. All this data is easily available online. You can go to Google and you can find out all the scores of all the countries on all the dimensions of the Geert Hofstede. So, for example, in this case, if we look at, for example, the power distance index, what we see is that the lowest score in the power distance index is of Germany and the highest is of China.

What does it mean? It simply means that in Germany the people do not accept the differences between the powerful people and the not so privileged people. So that gap between the haves and have-nots is not acceptable, at least culturally. I'm not saying that they are not rich people or they are not poor people. There are rich people and poor people, but society does not give any major or extra importance to a rich person or the fact that he has got better privileges in Germany. That does not happen. That is the meaning of this. So Germany's power distance score is the lowest. That is 35 below the average. And when we say average, we say the average is 50 because the scale is from 0 to 100 and 50 is average. That is assumed. It is definitely below the average 35. And definitely, it is more acceptable to the logic that power distance should not be there actually. And it is very high in the case of Brazil and China, as you can see here.

And if we look at the scores of the individualism versus collectivism of the Hofstede, we find that China has a very low score of 20 only and the US has a very, very high score of 91. Germany's score is also moderately high like the US and definitely it is above average. 67 is definitely above average. What is very, very clear is that China is a very, very collective society. So individuals do not have the kind of importance that the groups have in China. As a society, it is a highly collective society as against the very individualistic society like the US and the individualistic societies look for uniqueness, independence, freedom and non interference. They want the recognition of the individual person, not the group. The advancement of people in US companies is on an individual performance basis. While if we talk of China, China in China, you will find that the individual performance or the individual's performance is not that important. Rather, the particular group of people who are involved in a particular project and what is the outcome of the project will decide the rewards and compensation of the people working in Chinese companies. So that difference exists.

If we talk about masculinity versus femininity, we have talked a lot about it. These differences. What it indicates here very, very clearly is that the score of Germany and China is almost similar. That is 66 above average. It means the societies of China and Germany are very much masculine, if not extremely masculine. That actually is the case of Japan. Actually, we have not included Japan in this particular scheme. If we would have included Japan. It is a starkly very distinct culture, actually Japan. So we will talk about Japan maybe in the next chapters when we will compare Japanese culture with US culture. But here we see that the masculinity score is lowest for Brazil in this comparison. But let me tell you, in the world, the most feminine cultures are from Scandinavia. Countries like Sweden, Belgium, Luxembourg, Denmark, Scandinavian countries. Out there you will find these scores something like 20, 25, 30, very low scores, much below average.

So they are more feminine cultures and we have already discussed the differences wherein the slogan is that you live to work in the masculine culture, while in the feminine culture you work to live. So basically life is more important in feminine cultures than work. Now, at the same time, the United States also is more masculine out here, as you can see here, but definitely they are not as masculine as in the case of Japan. We will talk about it later in the next few chapters. Now coming to uncertainty avoidance, which means the propensity of taking risks or not taking risks or pre-planning in a very, very dexterous or religious manner to make sure that there are no awkward results, even if it means delays. So both sides have their positives and negatives. Whether uncertainty avoidance is high, has its advantages and disadvantages.

If uncertainty avoidance is low, it has its advantages and disadvantages. So, for example, if the uncertainty avoidance score is very low, which means cultures tend to take a lot of risks. High risk, high gain, for example, in this case, China is a country with below average score on the uncertainty avoidance. So in China, you will find the people are not afraid of failure. It clearly shows that when we compare with other countries, they are not afraid of failure. The score is very, very low. 30 is much below the average score, while in the case of Brazil, it is 76, and definitely still it is lower than the Japan case. Japan's UAI score is very high, but still, it is very high in Brazil. That indicates that people tend to be very, very sure whatever they are doing, that there is no awkward outcome of the things. And they would go to great extents to avoid any uncertainty in whatever they are doing. But that takes a toll on innovation. If failure is not acceptable, innovation will definitely go. So what do you think about your society, your culture? Do you think that the score of your country should be higher than the average or lower than the average? Just think about it and you can check the score of your country by googling and checking Hofstede's scores on the uncertainty avoidance, cultural dimension. Now long term versus short-term orientation of the societies.

When we compare Brazil, China, Germany, and the United States, we find that the most short term oriented country is the United States. As I had already given you the example of the Capitol Hill riots recently. That was a very unceremonious event and an avoidable thing. But it happened because of the instigation by one of the heads of the United States. And it was not in the good taste of a superpower like the USA. But the culture is like that. Culture itself is short term. So people think very short term. They do not look at things very objectively. They do not think that if they are getting involved in such kinds of riots at such an unprecedented level, in a very disappointing way, they have been attacking the Apex parliamentary building in the United States. So what is happening is that the people are very, very short thinking. But the score also says this. These scores have been developed over the years. So it clearly indicates the explanation of what actually transpired in the USA in the riots, recent riots, political riots.

At the same time, China's score is very, very high on the long-term orientation. At one time it was even more than 100. Initially, when this survey was done, it was realized that the score was more than 100 for China. It means it is actually the world's most long-term oriented culture. And you can easily see the Chinese reforms started in 1979 and continuously they have been working on infrastructure, research, innovation, and many, many things they have been working on, as the culture indicates, despite not getting the benefits, immediate benefits of whatever they were doing, they kept on working on that. And today, China has reached a stage where it can become a world superpower and the world new order may be China led actually. People are talking about that. And as far as the economy is concerned, it is soon going to surpass the US economy to become the number one economy in the world. So the long-term orientation of the culture indicates all these outcomes.

So many things are there in this particular chart, which I am giving you this example. And when you put your country here, look at the merits and demerits. Although let me tell you one thing, there is no such thing. There is nothing called merits and demerits in the cultures. Every culture has its own ways of doing things and they try to achieve excellence with whatever the profile of culture they have. So there is no single way of reaching success. So every country with whatever culture they have developed over many, many thousands of years, you really cannot change these cultural aspects overnight, the culture, whatever way they are. If you provide the right environment, they will definitely achieve success. So this is a fact. This we will talk about more later because that concerns our cross-cultural management aspect also. So when we manage different cultures, this fact should be very, very clear. And one theory is there that I will discuss in a very short time. The US versus China in this cultural dimension and the restraint versus indulgence.

Again, the USA is at the top with a very high score on indulgence, worldly indulgence, as I told you that even if they don't have money in their pocket, they will use their credit cards, but they will go on with their daily routine if they are used to. As against the highest score of the USA in indulgence, the lowest score in indulgence is of

China, which is 24. What does it mean? Again, Chinese society is diametrically different from US society when it comes to this dimension of indulgence. What we see here is that Chinese culture is highly restrained, which is also the case in Japan. We will compare Japan and the USA soon. You will see there. Japan is also a very restrained culture. On all these dimensions, we can definitely get some cues about what types of cultures are there on Geert Hofstede's scores and you will get an idea of the cultures of different countries and how to deal with them.

Country Wise Cultural Dimensions Scores Analysis On Examples Of 4

Now, if we talk about the cultural dimensions country wise, for example, if we look at Brazil, we'll start with Brazil as the first culture. We see that Brazil's scores are highest in power distance and in uncertainty avoidance and moderate to lower in other dimensions. So what is the meaning of this? The meaning of this is that Brazil as a culture is less individualistic, less masculine, less long term-oriented, but fairly above average when it comes to indulgence. So we can put this color here for this. So the score of Brazil in indulgence is also quite high. In three dimensions they display higher scores. That is power, distance, uncertainty, avoidance, and indulgence.

While they indicate low scores in individualism versus collectivism. And the long term orientation is not there. It is below average. That is the short-term thinking culture and it is more feminine because the score is almost average, we will say. So it's between the less masculine but more feminine. If we talk of China, we find that the Chinese society is very strong in power distance, masculinity and long-term orientation, but very low on individualism, which means it is more collective in nature. It is low in uncertainty avoidance. So it's a very risk taking kind of culture. And also it is very low on indulgence. So it's a very restrained culture. So when we see this, we find that Chinese culture has a very strong acceptability of the authority of certain people and highly masculine traits. Success, wealth, and power have a lot of meaning in this society, but they have a very long-term orientation. So they are ready to wait for the benefits of whatever they do on a very, very long-term basis. This is the way we can find out more about China.

If we talk of Germany, we find that Germany has very high scores on the long-term orientation. That is very interesting. When we compare it with the USA, it is very, very good and also it is fairly masculine. Above average. Individualism scores are also very high. Uncertainty avoidance is also very high. It means they are very particular about whatever they are doing and they probably are afraid of the failures. So they make sure that things are on the right track. And I'm not saying that it is a good thing, but that is what their culture is. Germany is very low, below average, at least in indulgence, and below average in power distance. So this also indicates the culture of Germany when we compare it with other countries. And it is very, very clear this type of society, which is not actually similar to the US, US culture is quite different actually.

If we look at the US culture, we find that US culture is very, very strong in terms of individualism, in terms of masculinity also, in terms of indulgence, it is very, very strong, but it is not strong actually, it is weak when it comes to power distance. So it is a positive thing actually if it is not accepting the importance of certain privileged people, which is actually indicative of very strong democracy actually, and low on uncertainty avoidance also. So it is a very risk-taking kind of society, but they are very short-term thinkers, so they are not strong in the long term thinking orientation. So that is what is the explanation of the United States. This is what, you know, is the way we analyze the scores. Geert Hofstede scores.

And I would strongly suggest that you use this chart and plot this chart, including your country also, and you make a comparison where you stand. You will find it very, very interesting. And if you want to include Japan in this, because Japan is a very distinct culture and it will give you a very good idea about your country if you share that particular image in the Q and A chapter of this Book, it will be very, very useful for the other students. And you can also analyze, you can give the analysis, your own analysis of your culture, and you can give a comment on your culture. Let me tell you, the profile of any culture cannot be treated as bad or good with this analysis. This analysis is only for business decision-making. How to do things. Something that you can do very well in one country by doing something based on that culture in another method, you can get the same result in another culture or another country by using some other methods. So the idea of this cultural comparison is to find the ways and means of managing and getting the best performance.

For example, in our case study of UNP, the US was involved, then Sweden was involved. Sweden is a very, very feminine kind of country, and we have not included it. A very, very low something like 15 - 20 score in masculinity versus femininity. Italy was also involved in that. It is not because of the culture. There are no implicit or inherent demerits of a culture. No culture is bad, actually. It is just that you should know how to manage and get the best results and that is what managers generally fail to do. So this is what I wanted to convey to you.

Comparing Japan and US cultures using Hofstede's cultural dimensions

So, friends, are you satisfied with the comparisons that I just did for four countries? Should we do some more comparisons? The comparison between Japanese culture and US culture is very, very important. I think there is still scope for comparing the culture of Japan and the US. My idea is that with these four countries that I just compared in the last chapter, this comparison between Japan and the US culture using the Hofstede score I think would be a very good idea to get a good hold on this particular model, because personally, my own opinion has been that the Hofstede's model is very, very popular, most widely used in businesses for taking business decisions.

So there is no harm, I think, in taking up the comparison of the culture between Japan and the US and it will only add to your confidence in this particular model and how you can use it. And definitely, you should try this model, this comparison with your country, with whichever country you want to compare. You have to find out. I think this kind of exercise will definitely help you. You will become very confident when it comes to cross-cultural management. So you not only compare cultures, but you get a lot of insights about the culture. And those insights actually give rise to several ideas and theories that I am going to take up after this comparison. Okay, So I think it will serve a very good purpose.

I will try to explain to you about Japanese culture. I will describe Japanese culture and how it is different from other cultures. So in this particular chapter, I will compare the cultural dimensions that were suggested by Geert Hofstede, the renowned researcher and scientist, in the cross-cultural comparison of the cultures of different countries as per the dimensions suggested by Geert Hofstede. I will compare

Japanese culture with the culture of the US. So you will find the scores of US culture in this column and Japanese culture. You will find the scores on different dimensions, mainly the Geert Hofstede cultural dimensions. I will explain and I will compare the scores of Japan with those of US if we talk about the cultural dimension, which is called uncertainty avoidance, meaning of which is that a higher score on uncertainty avoidance indicates a high level of avoidance of awkward results or uncertainty related to any action, any projects, any businesses.

The cultures with high uncertainty avoidance index scores display a high level of the pre-project work research and ensuring that everything is perfect. It is as per plan. There is no deviation in the implementation of the projects or business. The focus is on avoiding awkward results or negative results. So you will find that in this dimension, the score of Japanese culture is 92. When we compare the same score of American culture, US culture, the score of US culture is 46. As against the 46 score , the score of Japanese culture in uncertainty avoidance is extremely high. It is among the highest in the world. Because of this, there is a peculiarity, uniqueness in Japanese culture because that kind of deviation is not very common.

It is very rare. Looking at the second dimension suggested by Geert Hofstede and which is called the Power Distance Index, PDI, it is called in short, which indicates the acceptance of the hierarchical status of every individual in the society in a particular culture, how acceptable it is to the society, the existence of powerful people who dominate other people in society. They have got privileged status due to the existence of strong hierarchies in society. Higher scores indicate the existence of very, very strong hierarchical positions and the status of the individuals in the society. If we compare the Japanese cultural score on this dimension with that of the US. You find that in the US the score is much below average on PDI, which means that the US society is not really hierarchical, while in the case of Japan, it is somewhat hierarchical and you can say it is the borderline hierarchical society and definitely it is better than many other Asian societies.

The societies in the neighborhood like South Korea or China are much more hierarchical societies, the PDI scores of these countries are much higher than Japan. To that extent, we can say that Japanese culture is hierarchical from the Western standards, but perhaps not hierarchical from Asian standards. But the third dimension of Geert Hofstede is called the Masculinity versus Femininity index score. You find that Japanese culture is highly masculine. In fact, it is the most masculine culture in the world. And if we compare this score with the US culture, that actually should be masculine because of the high level of individualism in American culture. Still, the score of the US is just 62, while the score of Japanese culture is 95. What it indicates that there is a higher level of competition among the people in Japan, but this particular aspect of competition among the individual does not exist in Japan because of the high level of pluralism, because of the existence of the collective society, because of the low score on the individualism index in the fourth dimension of Geert Hofstede that compared with the US, is much lower because in the US culture, the individualism index score of Geert Hofstede is 91. To a greater extent, Japanese society is collective in nature and competition still exists because of the high level of masculinity in Japan among the groups, the companies, among the business houses.

So that competition is extremely high because of which Japanese culture is regarded as the most masculine culture in the world. The fifth dimension of Geert Hofstede refers to the LTO score which is the long-term orientation. We find again that the score of Japanese culture, when compared with US culture, is extremely high. In fact, the score of US culture is much lower on this dimension, the meaning of which is that the Japanese culture is highly long-term oriented and their actions and their planning and their slow decision making. There are so many aspects of the culture that are visible and which indicate the long-term planning of the Japanese companies, including the focus on the market share rather than on the quarterly or year to year profits of the companies. So there are many, many aspects that I will discuss in a little more detail later. But this is a very important dimension of the culture that makes the Japanese culture very unique when compared with other cultures of the world.

Now, finally, the sixth dimension of the Geert Hofstede framework of the cultural dimensions, the comparison of the cultures of different countries, and that is the indulgence score that indicates the extent to which a society tends to restrain their inherent desires and impulses and tries to restrict their desires and impulses to indulge in worldly comforts and actions that may not be socially acceptable in many other cultures. So we find that the score of Japanese culture on the indulgence index is lower than the average, while if we compare with the US culture where the indulgence level is much higher. So I will talk in a little more detail about this particular dimension and what it means for the Japanese culture, because I want to really spend a good amount of time on making you understand that what are the uniqueness of the Japanese culture because that is the most important aspect of dealing with Japan, and that's a very major success or failure factor when doing business with Japan.

Then finally, if we talk about the context of the culture, we find that Japanese culture is a high context culture when we compare it with the US culture, that is a low-context culture. So what you find is that in a high context culture, society works on the inherent rules and regulations that need to be understood. They need not be communicated verbally. While in the case of low context culture, people manage their societies and day-to-day life with a lot of communication, verbal expressions, and verbal disBooks. It is easier to understand the low context culture. It is much more difficult to understand the high-context culture for outsiders. So that actually creates a lot of challenges and barriers for outsiders to be successful in Japan. But with the proper understanding of Japanese culture, it is possible to succeed in Japanese culture.

The efforts of the Japanese government in present times and the overall resolve of the Japanese society to accept the outsiders and the cultures of the world at present is making it much easier for the outsiders to operate in Japan.

Conclusion

So, friends, we studied a lot of very important information in this module and we now definitely know that it is definitely possible to draw good inferences about the cultural traits of high context or the low context in different varying extents, because there is nothing called the highest context or there is nothing called the lowest context it can be in between. There is no black and white. It is the grays actually. Using the high context or low context cultural mapping of different nations it is definitely possible to draw good inferences.

We also learned in this module that Hofstede's cultural dimension model is one of the most popular and widely used tools to compare national cultures and see the cultural differences. We wanted to talk about the Globe Project in this module, but we shifted this particular topic to the next module that talks of leadership because it is more pertinent to talk about the leadership, preferred leadership styles in different countries. So that's why we did not talk about the Globe project that actually can be included in this module also, but we prefer to move that topic to the next module that will be taken up in the next module.

These models that are discussed in this module can definitely help managers increase their cross-cultural competence for effective leadership and the appropriate dealing and managing of multicultural teams. So these multicultural groups have to be managed efficiently, requiring certain skills and competencies which can definitely be obtained through these very, very popular models that we discussed in this module. These cultural dimension models definitely can help in taking important strategic international business decisions. So we are on the same page on this point that all these models are definitely useful and they are very easy to use in fact. Because the scores and data are easily available online and you can easily find them free of cost.

And then finally, similar ideas can also be used to manage multicultural remote teams that I talked about. I told you about the current situation, the current global challenges that humans are facing, after the Covid pandemic. Work from home culture has resulted in a very large number of organizations embracing the work-from-home culture, and it is going to remain for many, many years to come. Those remote teams, the multicultural teams, require similar ideas with some new knowledge, and new experiences that I will definitely be updating in this Book in the very near future.

Management Skills Training for New & Experienced Managers

Now friends in the next module that refers to leadership, management style and national cultures, we have very pertinent questions like when a successful leader changes a country. And thus he gets into a different culture. What in his leadership does he have to adapt and what has to be retained or what has to be maintained from the home culture? So these are the questions that come to our mind, which we are going to address in this module.

And questions like whether the effectiveness of a certain leadership style is influenced by cultural differences. So are there certain preferred leadership styles in the local cultures that produce outstanding leadership? Or at least can we understand the perception of the people of the local people, local cultures, that which type of leadership and leadership traits are more effective to them? Now questions like, Are there universal qualities also in a leader that are appreciated equally by the followers all over the world? So are there any common traits that actually are revered by all cultures? So if they are there, then the focus on such traits will be very, very helpful, especially in identifying the most competent global business managers and the competent intercultural managers, intercultural communicators. Or the question arises that is it that things are even more complicated than what we are talking about?

Are there more complexities involved in understanding the relationship between the leadership styles or the management styles and the local national cultures? So what kind of organization, culture, and therefore management styles, the management around the world follow? Can we identify those typical management styles of different countries? Are they really helpful? Are they going to help us in improving our cross-cultural competence? So these are the things which we will try to look into, in this particular module. Are these management styles affected by the implicit preferred leadership styles by the dominant local cultures? So this is also a very, very important question to be talked about that we will be definitely doing in this module. These are the types of questions that we are going to take up in this particular module.

Issues Related To Leadership Styles In Cross Cultural Management

Hello, friends. Welcome back, friends. We have already talked about the ways of understanding the cultural differences among the nations, and we have discussed several models, cultural models that actually help us to understand these differences. And we have also discussed certain theories that help us in understanding the ways we can do cross-cultural management. But there is still one aspect. Don't you think that it is also very important and it should matter? That is, the leadership, the leadership style.

What do you think about the case study, the opening case study of this Book about UNP, Did you see any leadership failure anywhere? Did you see any gaps with respect to leadership? These are the things that we still want to discuss in this Book so that we have an understanding of the role of leadership in managing the different national cultures and cultural differences. These discussions should be able to give us some insights into how to carry out cross-cultural management in situations like what transpired in the UNP case, but many similar situations. What are the possible issues that are related to leadership in different cultures? So that is to be understood. So some of the issues thus come to mind are expectations of the followers from the leader, which means the employees who have certain expectations depending on their national culture, because they have a different belief system, they have different behavior, they have a different attitude. And different values.

So because of these different parameters, different cultures, obviously their expectations would be different about the attributes and characteristics, personal characteristics of the leader. So those expectations have to be understood. Then the second issue comes to the nature and quality of the leader and the follower. That is the subject's interaction and the exchange of information, exchange of ideas, and Of course the relationship between the leader and the subjects. So that is the second issue. The third issue which comes to mind is the ability of the leaders and especially foreign leaders, somebody from a different culture to be able to adapt to the local culture, local expectations and the profile of the local subjects, the followers.

And the fourth thing that comes to mind is about identifying the most effective leadership styles in a specific country. So if we take the example of UNP for Upjohn's managers to identify effective ways of leading the employees of the Swedish group as well as the Italian groups, So what are those effective leadership styles? Is there any way to understand that? And the fifth point which comes to mind in this direction relates to the ability of the leaders to fine-tune the practices of leadership or leading or administering the culturally different workforce for a specific leadership approach to the local values and preferences. Local values, belief systems, attitude and behavior. So is it possible to fine tune?

Is it possible to have those capabilities in the leader and to be able to identify such leaders in the organization that can do this kind of fine-tuning of the practices, looking at and observing the local values and preferences? And the sixth point that comes to mind in this regard is the ability of the leaders to build a suitable local corporate culture. So, for example, was it possible for Upjohn's managers in the case study which we discussed to build an acceptable and expected local corporate culture? The islands of the local corporate culture in the Swedish group and the Italian groups. Was it possible? And finally, what comes to mind? The seventh point. Is the ability of the leaders to be able to manage diversity, especially in foreign cultures, foreign cultural groups. These are some of the questions that come to mind when we are talking of the impact of leadership on managing cultural differences.

So do you agree with these questions? That looks like a very logical and obvious question. When we are trying to understand cross-cultural management and the ways of managing such situations that were encountered in the case of the UNP. So what do you think? What are your views? Write it down. Write it as the questions, in the Q and A chapter of this Book.

Leader-Member-Exchange (LMX) Theory

So, friends, one of the simplest theories, but a very popular theory in this respect is called the LMX theory. That is the leader member exchange theory. What is the concept of this theory? The concept of this theory focuses on the quality of the relationship between the leader and the members of the team. It becomes even more important, actually, when the leader is from a different culture, different cultural background. Whether he is able to really build a relationship of high quality between himself or herself with the subjects or the members of the culturally different teams. Is it possible?

Does he have that capability? And is it possible to really create that? So what are the ways of doing it? How to do it requires a lot of knowledge, that is what we are trying to understand in this Book. The influence of the members on the leader, especially in a cross-cultural situation, is very, very important when it comes to understanding the theory. What actually is the impact of the leader-member exchange interaction and the ensuing influence of the members of the leader. What does he grasp from that kind of interaction, especially in this different, culturally different situation, cross-cultural situation? So in this theory, the efforts are to be directed to boost the high quality of the leader-member exchange based on trust, liking loyalty and mutual respect.

So that is the idea of this theory. This theory is very subjective in nature. It actually depends on the situation, but it is very important and it is a very good starting point for understanding the role of leadership in being able to effectively manage cross-cultural situations.

Culturally Endorsed Implicit Leadership Theory (CLT) - Part 1

Friend. What do you think is the nature of the expectations of the follower? What triggers the expectations? What recreates, and what shapes the expectations of the followers? What are the dimensions that make up this expectation? So one of the theories, implicit leadership theory. I will talk about a very, very popular and very famous theory that explains the expectations of the followers according to which these are the implicit influence of the national cultures based on unique values, unique beliefs, unique behavior and unique attitude of the different cultures of the world. So what actually is this implicit influence?

It is nothing but out of conscious awareness and expectations of the followers about the preferred personal characteristics and attributes of the leader, and especially a leader who comes from a different national background. So it doesn't matter which national background it comes from. But is he able to understand the expected unconscious, that is very, very important because it is not conscious. So followers will not be able to tell the leader what they want. Even if the leader wants to talk to the subjects, the followers, what they want, they will not be able to tell it. This is out of conscious awareness, which means even the followers do not express this and are unable to express it. That is very important.

Do you think that out of conscious awareness will be able to help the followers to tell the leader what they want from the leader? Is it speakable? Is it communicable? So what do you think? These are the expectations that are implicit in nature. And that's why it is called implicit leadership theory. And this theory is actually very, very famous, and that is called the Globe study. What is the Globe study?

The Globe study is about universal leadership preferences. So the study was started several years before by House and his fellow Scientists. What they did, they were trying to search for outstanding leadership styles in different cultures of the world. So they wanted to map the different characteristics and attributes of the leaders who are required for outstanding leadership styles in different countries. So what they did, they studied 112 different behavioral and attribute descriptors like diplomacy, being able to inspire or tender, determined many, many different types of behavior and attribute descriptors that may contribute to or may impede the formation of outstanding leadership, effective leadership in different national cultures, and in different countries.

So that was the search and the main lead author of this study, House and his researchers in the study identified out of these 112 behavioral and attribute descriptors, six global leadership dimensions, which they found plays the maximum role in contributing to or impeding the creation of outstanding leadership in different countries. So they created scores from 0 to 7 on these six global leadership dimensions which are also called the leadership dimensions. That means culturally endorsed implicit leadership theory. So CLT leadership dimensions, it is called.

Culturally Endorsed Implicit Leadership Theory (CLT) - Part 2

So these six dimensions, those were identified by Globe Project for assessing the CLT across the global cultures. I just tell you, that CLT means culturally endorsed leadership traits. These six identified cultural dimensions of Globe study are the charismatic, value based leadership. One CLT dimension that tends to inspire, motivate and expects high performance from others on the basis of firmly held core values. The ability to understand those core values, especially in a culturally different situation, in a cross-cultural situation is a very, very difficult task, and it really requires a charismatic and value based leadership. So core values based leadership firmly held core values. That is very, very important in this.

The second dimension, leadership dimension, CLT dimension is team-oriented leadership which emphasizes the effective team building and implementation of a common goal. Being able to build that team that requires this type of leadership, team-oriented leadership. And the third dimension is participative leadership. That is the degree that managers involve others in making or implementing the decisions. So what kind of participative involvement is there of the members of the team along with the leader? That degree indicates the level of participative leadership. The fourth CLT leadership dimension is humane-oriented leadership, which actually is humane and supportive. So the degree of humaneness and supportive nature of the leader, that type of leadership refers to the humane oriented leadership. And the fifth one is autonomous leadership which signifies independent leadership.

How independent and autonomous the leader is, how much he is dependent on the team, how much he is dependent on the organization. So these things are covered in this kind of autonomous leadership. And finally, the sixth CLT leadership dimension is self-protective leadership which focuses on ensuring the security of the individual or group members, even if it requires certain decisions, certain controversial decisions. The focus remains on ensuring the security of the individual, the leader himself or herself and the group members. So in certain cultures, this is important.

In another culture, something else is important or a combination of different dimensions is there. So for most of the countries, the main countries, Globe study found scores from 0 to 7 on these six dimensions. Those actually help in understanding the leadership style differences among the countries. So this project is really, really helpful and it is one of the most authoritative research studies, a very long study done on thousands of managers and thousands of companies across the world. This CLT theory culturally endorsed implicit leadership theory. Dimensions six dimensions are charismatic, team-oriented, participative, humane, autonomous, self Protective. So if we take the example of Mexico and Germany, we find that the scores from 0 to 7 for Mexico are given here for all the six dimensions as well as for Germany.

It is possible to find these scores for any country. So if we take the example of our UNP case study, we can find similar scores for the US, Sweden and Italy. The scores above four generally signify that these attributes of the CLT dimensions contribute to the outstanding leadership and scores below four tend to impede outstanding leadership. This is generally the explanation given for these scores. So, for example, in our own case, if we look at the scores of US, Sweden, and Italy, we find that the scores of Sweden and Italy, as far as the dimensions are concerned, are almost the same, actually. The average scores are absolutely the same in the case of Sweden and Italy, but they are very much different on the charismatic dimension. Participative dimension. Human dimension and self-protective dimension.

When we compare the Swedish scores with US or we compare the Italian scores with US and we see these significant differences on these dimensions. So these score differences definitely indicate the friction, the differences, the implicit expectations from the leader of the Swedish group and the Italian group from the US managers. So this requires good study by the leaders so that the inferences from these scores can be used for effective cross-cultural management by the companies hailing from the US and being able to manage cross-cultural management in countries like Sweden, Italy or other countries. So in our UNP case, definitely these scores can be used to draw certain inferences for the leaders if they want to do effective cross-cultural management and avoid the kind of fiasco that took place in UNP. So do you really see the benefits of these scores in the UNP case?

What is your opinion if you look at these scores? Do you see the relationship between these scores with the Hofstede Cultural Dimensions model? So those relationships you can analyze definitely. And if you want to compare your country with the US or many other countries, you can create this kind of table. You can write down all these six CLT dimensions and you can find the scores for your country and you compare those scores with the other countries like you did in the Hofstede model. So this is a very, very useful model, and these scores are easily available online. You can easily find these scores for all the countries.

Building A Global Corporate Culture Based on Ethical Behavior

Now, friends, we have a fairly good idea that leadership has an impact on cross-cultural management and there are issues that are related to leadership. So what do you think? Do you think that leadership plays a very important role? If you have some ideas about the other issues related to leadership that are not covered in this Book, do share your ideas in the Q and A chapter so that those ideas can be included in the Book later on. But in the meantime, there are certain more issues that I want to discuss and they relate to building of the global corporate culture and that too, based on ethical behavior. So don't you think that in the case of UNDP, if very professional work would have been done on creating a global culture based on ethical values which are suitable to the culture of the US, to the culture of Sweden, to the culture of Italy, if that had been created, do you feel that things would have been different? So let us discuss that issue.

Building a global corporate culture and ethical behavior in a cross-cultural environment is a very challenging task which requires highly trained people. You will soon start appreciating that after completion of this cross-cultural management Book, you will find it is not difficult to get fully trained people who specialize in managing such a cross-cultural environment. So those global leadership traits are available at a premium, but they are available. How much can a premium person with those kinds of skills spend $1 billion? For example, in the case of UNP, those kinds of costs require the right people even if they are available on premium.

So this cross-cultural management Book can create such premium people who are available in the market, who know cross-cultural management. They have a 360-degree view of the issues which are involved in such a kind of cross-cultural management. So that is the purpose of this Book. So the building of a global corporate culture and ethical behavior in a cross-cultural environment requires an ethical global leadership that spearheads and builds the core global culture of the organization and protects it. That is the objective, in my view. What do you think about it? Do share in the Q and A chapter of this Book. In my view, a global culture cannot be built with anything less than ethical leadership and ethical behavior. It is not possible.

What actually happens, and probably that is what actually happened in the UNP case is also the difference in the cultures as perceived by the management and in this case of UNP, when I say management, I mean the parent company. That is UpJohn and the practices of multicultural workers. In this case, I am talking of workers of Swedish origin and Italian origin. And Of course, in a multicultural environment, the US workers are also included in this. So what are the practices, cultural practices, for example, in Sweden? What are the practices in Italy? What are the practices in the US? So those multicultural workers' practices and the difference as perceived by the management can create conflict and ethical issues can also arise in this. For example, in the UNP case, these were not just ethical issues, these were also issues of lost morale, disgruntled employees.

Somewhere the question of ethics comes into their mind and without the question of ethics, the morale of the employees will not go down. Somewhere they will feel that the organization is not acting ethically. That is what actually comes first in the mind. That is the reason in the UNP case, some of the key talents left the company in spite of the fact that they were loyal to the company. These ethical issues came to their mind definitely. That is the reason they left and joined other companies. So without these issues arising, it cannot happen. The ethical part should not be forgotten in such cases. That is very, very important, actually.

Building the core ethical values can be done by rewarding the ethical behavior and punishing the transgression, but very carefully. In a cross-cultural environment, how do you punish the transgressions, requires a lot of brainstorming. Parent company actually has to be very, very sensitive when they are being judgmental about other cultures. So this punishment actually has to come from the leadership of the local culture only. The local people, and the local leadership only should be able to punish such transgressions, if any. And that reinforces the faith in the ethical, corporate, global culture. The punishment, organization wide, world wide, which may include, for example, in the UNP case, the US workers also, it could be Swedish workers, Italian workers. But how to initially manage this issue of rewarding and punishing in other cultures, that is, the Swedish culture or the Italian culture in this case, has to be done very tactfully. So again, that tactfully means on ethical grounds only.

So giving the right signals to the workers that whatever is being done is being done in the core objective of maintaining and protecting the core ethical values of the organization. And then, Of course, all these efforts have to be supported by ethics programs. The programs and practices in the organization maintain the ethical culture, ethical global culture in the organization on a worldwide scale. This kind of leadership can build the global corporate culture and ethical behavior in this kind of cross-cultural environment. A multicultural environment is a very, very specialized task, but it is very, very important. So the building of an ethical, global corporate culture is very, very important. And work on this has to start at the very beginning of the merged organization or any other kind of interaction that is taking place in the organization on an international level for international trade or for alliances or for joint ventures, whatever may be the situation, these issues will definitely emerge. And there the role of worldwide global leadership, capable leadership, cultural awareness, cultural competency all these things will matter.

Managing Worldwide Diversity

Now, friends, another angle to look at this issue is the ability of the leaders and the managers to be able to manage the diversity in a cross-cultural environment. How do they do it? That becomes another issue. What do you think of the worldwide diversity, can it be managed by a handful of managers from the parent company or it has to be managed on a local level by the managers at the local units? For example, in the UNP case in the Swedish group or in the Italian group? Certain managers have to be brought on board to be able to manage diversity. What do you think? Your views? Please share your views on this issue.

As per the research and the practices in the organizations, what has emerged in the literature and in the research papers that diversity management on a global scale starts with the global definition of diversity or the definition of global diversity, national cultures, and diversity. So what is required is to correctly redefine and recognize all kinds of diversity. It is not just about national diversity. Saying that the Swedish group is there, the Italian group is there in the UNP case, and then US workers are also involved. So in UNP there are three types of groups, but there can also be diversity on gender issues. There can be diversity from other angles. Maybe in the Swedish group and the Italian group, there are workers from other nationalities also. So those minority groups cannot be ignored. Depending on the situation you have to define the major, minor, hidden, open, and all kinds of diversities.

And depending on the situation, this diversity can take different forms and names. So the second step in this diversity management is to redefine discrimination. So what are the areas where discrimination on national cultures or on the issues that are related to the national cultures or the issues which are related to multicultural workplaces or the issues related to the parent and subsidiary companies relationship? For example, in the UNP case, there can be different types of discrimination which are possible that have the potential to create dissatisfaction among the employees, especially of the different culture employees of the companies that have been acquired.

The parent company managers can hide the discrimination which can actually eat away at the performance of the employees of the other cultures. You have to identify and redefine discrimination so redefine discrimination and clampdown on all its forms. So that is also very, very important and it has to be done very sensitively. So we will discuss at the end of this Book by giving you several ways and means of using these kinds of techniques of how the UNP case could have been dealt with to avoid the situation that was faced by UNP so that we will do it later. But for now, you have to understand that this discrimination identification is important and especially cultural discrimination.

The third very important aspect of diversity management relates to the celebration of diversity. Now, this is a very strong position. Can you really celebrate diversity? Can you think of the ways the companies, especially the managers of the parent company, can find ways and means of celebrating diversity, especially multicultural diversity, multicultural workplaces? Right? In the case of, for example, UNP, there were 35,000 employees of the merged entity. The employees were from not only US, Sweden, and Italy, but from other nationalities also. Are we able to convey the message to all the workforce across the worldwide presence of the organization that the organization is there to celebrate diversity, whether major or minor. All diverse groups in the organization are welcome in the organization. An organization is ready to celebrate their presence.

You have to find, the leadership has to find all possible ways of celebrating diversity. How they do it will depend on the situation. Some kinds of budgets may be required. Some kinds of celebrations of festivals of all cultural groups are required. How do you institutionalize those celebrations of the different festivals of the different minority or majority groups, cultural groups? National cultural groups? Keeping track of all the possible opportunities where diversity can be celebrated is a very, very innovative process, and the right leadership can do it. It is not difficult to do it. It is doable.

Another very, very important aspect of this kind of global diversity management, cultural diversity management is finding the ways and means of reaching out to all the interest groups, all the cultural groups. Whether major, minor, hidden, open, of all departments, all part of the organization, in all countries, wherever the presence of the organization is there. How do you reach out? You have to find out the ways. The leadership needs to find out the ways, not only find out the ways their next job is to keep reaching out to the people.

The people should not be left. The minority groups should not be left behind. Identify the minority cultural groups. It is important and this kind of leadership is the need of cross-cultural management. And finally, a very important aspect, the managers and the leaders, especially of the parent company, should not assume that whatever they gossip, whatever they convey in meetings or at any other event of the organization, any kind of official engagement, they should not assume that whatever they speak about the other cultures or the minority groups or the diverse groups, that people will take it as a joke.

In an organization, once you communicate something, it can result in big problems. Same thing happened in the UNP case. The small things escalated and the result of which was that in less than a decade, the names of all the organizations involved vanished from the market.

Small, loose talks or small jokes about other cultures can escalate into big issues. So those assumptions a good leader, a good global leader will never do. What do you think this kind of diversity management can be expected of the most effective global leaders? Do you think that there are many other things that can be done for diversity management by such leaders? If you think so, do share your ideas.

Leadership and Management Styles - Part 1

So, friends, do you think that the leadership styles, as explained in CLT theory, the CLT dimensions, do you think that it will have a direct impact on the way management is run in different countries, the management styles in different countries? So what is your opinion on this? I think you will appreciate that CLT dimensions are implicit dimensions. While the management styles are affected by not only the preferred leadership and that is unconscious leadership preferences. So in the conscious mind, there are cultural differences among countries, even in the European continent, in different European countries, you find a lot of cultural differences, as explained by the Hofstede model. The management styles in different countries are not only affected by cultural factors, the cultural differences, but are also affected by the history of the country, the infrastructure, the environment.

Many, many factors that are there in those countries. And for that reason, although leadership does play an important role in explaining management styles, the management style differences cannot be understood using any theories like globe research or Hofstede model. Those facilities, those tips, and techniques cannot be used. So in such a case, it is important to understand the features, salient features, and the characteristics of the management styles in these countries. That is my view. What do you think? If you think there can be some ways of understanding the management styles in different countries? If you have any ideas, do share. As per my understanding, it is important to understand those management styles, typical management styles, features and characteristics in those countries.

For some of the countries, I will just explain to you some of the salient features, the summary of the typical management styles. For example, if we talk about Germany, where the management style is more of a hierarchy plus consensus, in Germany, the typical management styles are characterized by a clear chain of command. It means there is a hierarchy, but it does not mean there is no consensus. So considerable value is placed on consensus building. That's why this management style in Germany is called the hierarchy plus consensus management style. So in Germany, managers seem at all levels striving for excellence, and perfection in processes and procedures. If any manager is looking at those perfections, that excellence is supposed to be a person who has a strong liking for the existing system in Germany and the rewards are given to such managers. So that is a general situation in Germany. And you find a good level of solidarity among managers and workers. So in other words, the status of workers and managers is very equal, its single status, while in many other countries you will find a lot of distinctions between the managers and the workers.

Like, for example, in Italy. In Germany, you find a fair amount of solidarity among the managers and the workers. But the managers normally work long hours. They tend to follow and obey rules. They focus on fair play, a justified working style is there in Germany and they are always ready to welcome instructions from their superiors. So this is the typical management style that prevails in Germany. So similar styles exist in many countries with some variations. So I will keep on giving you some more examples of some of the countries where I will explain to you the salient features and characteristics of the typical management styles in those countries. Similar information you can gather for almost all countries. If we talk of the typical management style in France, that is generally an autocratic way of management style. So autocratic management style prevails in France. This is generally observable and decisions are generally taken at the top.

Orders are generally communicated across the organization in a tops-down manner, which means the decisions taken at the top are informed throughout the hierarchy, moving from top to bottom. So that's why it is a tops down approach. And out there in France, generally, ultimate success is often less important than heroics in carrying out projects. What happens because of the history of France, of the people having pride in their history, of the likes of Napoleon, who might have failed, but his heroics are still liked by such cultures. So that still prevails in France. And that's why you see this kind of situation, which actually is more focused on the heroics rather than the ultimate success.

What happens in France, there is a high tolerance for the manager's blunders also. So that's quite weird and strange, but it is there. So interdependence, however, with mutual tolerance and teamwork, is very, very common in France. And French employees generally have faith in the appointed leaders and managers. So these were the typical characteristics and features of the management style in France.

Leadership and Management Styles - Part 2

Now, friends, talking of the typical management style of Japan, which is ringi-sei consensus, generally it is referred to as. So the management style in Japan is characterized by Confucian hierarchy, which means the authority is there at the top. Definitely it is there. But the same is also characterized by the fact that the top management, the top managers generally do not play any major role in day-to-day working or everyday affairs. So their involvement is very, very less in day-to-day affairs. So they do occasionally initiate policies after getting the consensus and getting the recommendations from the bottom on such policies.

And they really take time to initiate such policies. So occasionally they appear for such roles to initiate policies once they are built on the ideas and suggestions from the bottom and approved by many, many people in the organization. So their role comes at that point. Obviously, a large number of people are involved in policy formulation in Japan. The ratification of the policy at the top at the right time is done and conveyed across the organization. So there is a process involved from the bottoms up approach and then tops down approach. So this cyclical way of decision-making is most common in Japan. If we talk about the typical management styles that are prevalent in Spain, these are generally referred to as the human force. So they are very different types of management styles actually, where the human attributes and human influence plays a very, very important role.

Do you see in these different management styles that I have just mentioned, the echo of the type of management styles that exist in your own country, So you should try to find out. And if you want to share a similar account of the management style, the typical management style in your country, do share with me or with the group in the Q and A chapter, but just mention the country of origin along with your account that you share with other fellow students. So the human force management style of Spain is characterized by autocratic but charismatic leadership. So here the leadership does affect the management style that exists in Spain, and the decisions made by the managers are often not based on pure logic, but rather on intuitions. So again, the echoes of the human force are here. So intuition is there. Then focus on personal influence and human force that I just mentioned to you is very much there in the management style in Spain, where employees are motivated by the managers because of the personal influence and the aura of the human force exerted by the managers on the employees.

So what it means is that the style of working in Spain is declamatory in nature, theatrical in nature. So that is what it is in Spain. And generally, the decisions made by the managers are supposed to be irreversible. So it is not expected that the managers would be forced to reverse their decisions. So because it is autocratic, because it is charismatic, because it is declamatory in nature and because it is characterized by personal influence and human force, the typical management style of Spain is very, very unique in nature. Okay, If we are talking of the typical management style of Sweden, it is very, very important for us because our opening case study involved three geographic regions, US, Sweden, and Italy. So it will be very, very important for us to understand typical management styles in these regions. Talking about Sweden, that is also part of the opening case study.

The management style in Sweden is Primus inter pares. This means it is a democratic style of working with flat hierarchies and fewer layers of hierarchy. So it is not a tall hierarchy. It is mostly the vertical hierarchy and the managers in Swedish management styles are easily accessible. They are ready to support. They are always ready to guide. They are very much available for any support that is required by the employees. And typically there is a Swedish law also that stipulates that in companies based in Sweden, the important decisions should be based on the suggestions of many people and the overall consensus building. So that law is there, which is very, very typical of Sweden. It also indicates the way management is carried out. Management operations are carried out in Sweden, which is also very unique.

Leadership and Management Styles - Part 3

Now, friends, our focus on the USA is very much there because we have been talking about the parent company, Upjohn, that acquired the Pharmacia of Sweden, which had already acquired Farmitalia of Italy. So it is very, very important for us to understand the typical management style of the US. So whatever knowledge which we are gaining in this Book with respect to leadership, with respect to the cultural differences, identification of them, and the different theories that we are going to discuss in this Book about cross-cultural management, all these kinds of tips and techniques and methods will give you skills that, coupled with the knowledge of the typical management style in the countries involved, the major cultural groups coming from these countries involved, it will become reasonably comfortable and doable for you to effectively manage the situations like what we discussed about in the UNP case study.

US management style the focus is mainly on getting the things done. This is again a very unique type of management style where the top managers are supposed to get the

job done by whatever means, and generally, they try to find shortcuts for success, for making money, for getting more profits for the organization, and to allow the possibility of monetary benefits to the employees because the money speaks in US. So CEOs are expected to act and they definitely enjoy a lot of authority and they seldom fail to act actually, because they have to get things done. And whatever is required to get things done, they can take reBook to any extent to any tacts in order to get the job done.

The motivation of the employees in US management styles mostly comes from the monetary rewards rather than any other things. So that is very, very typical of it. But at the same time, the managers are very capable in the working of the US companies because the managers, if they are not capable, are generally fired very fast. So hire and fire is a very, very common thing in the US management style. But at the same time, these capable managers expect complete independence and freedom that remains the focus across the organization from the lower level to the top level so that independence and freedom is very, very important and that becomes the leadership style also along with the management style in the USA. Finally, we are talking about the management styles in Italy and Of course, Italy is another focus area for us to understand for this Book because we are discussing the opening case study of UNP, where Italy is also one of the regions that is involved in the finding of the solution to the problem discussed in that. The Italian management style is characterized by pyramidal hierarchy.

So that is very, very typical again, of Italy. So you must have noticed then when we are talking about the typical management styles of different countries, the styles are not very similar in the countries. So you will find these styles are unique to each country because of the unique cultures of the world, because of the presence of many factors involved in developing the management style. So that's why you will find that no two countries will have very similar management styles and you will find a lot of differences as far as the management styles are concerned. And that is the reason there is no single way of categorizing such management styles and the individual country has to be discussed for this purpose. So pyramidal hierarchy is the main feature of the Italian typical management style and the final decisions are normally centralized at the top.

So being a pyramidal hierarchy, Of course, the approach is a top-down approach in the Italian management style. But there exists among the employees great respect for the supervisors, managers, and bosses. So that is there. And generally, a consensus is expected on the decisions and it is normally available in the management style of Italy. But at the same time, the style of working is team-oriented and participative in nature. So this is the typical management style of Italy. And you can see if we compare the management styles of US, Sweden and Italy, which we had discussed earlier, also in this Book. But here we have given in very more general terms. So you do see differences in the management styles and that is what was in play and that had to be managed somehow.

So this Book focuses on the ways and means and the approaches that have to be used for such kinds of cross-cultural management. So now, before closing on this particular unit of the Book that talks about leadership and the management styles in different countries, let us close by comparing the management styles in Japan and US in a more detailed manner so that this will serve as a demonstration to you that how you can compare two different countries with each other as far as the management styles are concerned and the similar way you can do for your own country also. And if you do something similar, do share it with the other students of this Book and write and share your notes on the Q and A chapter or send it to me. I will put it in the Q and A chapter for the benefit of the students. Or I can put your ideas if they are with merit in the Book itself, in the resource chapter of the Book also. That can be done. In the next chapter, we will start with the comparison of management styles in Japan with the US.

Comparing Japan And Us Management Styles - Part 1

So friends, if we compare Japanese and US management features, the characteristics of the management system that works there. If we talk about aspects like lifetime employment, that is actually quite high in Japan, and it is very low in the US. So people are not working in US companies for lifetime employment and the employers in the US are not giving lifetime employment. But it is not the case in Japan which traditionally has this system of providing lifetime employment. They take care of the employees.

The welfare of the employees is very good and the systems are created in such a way that the people work with the organization for lifetime. Although in very recent times, let me tell you, we are very clear with you that these characteristics are now diluting. The line between these differences is blurring now. But still, these features you can easily see when you work with Japan. The second aspect is about the discrimination. So in general, there is no discrimination on caste or any race. Those things are not there in Japan, but there is discrimination on gender. So the discrimination in favor of the males and not in favor of the females are there. And let me tell you, it is generally said by the experts that the reason why Japanese companies discriminate against women is because they generally have this idea that women will not work for them for a lifetime. So they will leave the companies if they are married or if they move from one city to another city or for various reasons, they have the practical reality that they generally face that women leave the organization which they don't like.

Actually, the system does not like that thing. So the main reason for the discrimination, as the experts have found out, is because of this reason and this discrimination does exist. So you can say that the level of discrimination in Japanese companies is medium, while in the case of the US companies it is very low. But in the US it generally complains that there do exist racism and discrimination against the black people. So that part is there in the US. But Of course you cannot compare apples and oranges. They are two different things. But in general, if we talk about the expert's opinion, yes, discrimination exists in the Japanese system on a moderate scale, while it is very low in US companies. So why I'm talking about these differences is because most of the people are aware of the ways of doing business in the US or in some English-speaking European countries. So a comparison of these parameters, on the main management features, when we compare Japan and the US, will definitely help you to understand the Japanese market.

Now if we talk about the third dimension of the Japanese management features that we are comparing with the US, if we look at the recruitment procedures. So in the Japanese management system, the Japanese management feature is that the recruitment procedure of the Japanese HR department is very, very rigorous for the simple reason they are looking for the cream and cream only. The best companies in Japan look for cream so that they will do a lot of churning, interviews, and several interviews to be absolutely sure that the person who is being recruited is the best. It also emanates from the high score of uncertainty avoidance, as you know that the Japanese score on the Japanese cultural score on high uncertainty avoidance is very, very high. So they do not want any bad results or awkward results. They will take a lot of time to decide and work out things.

And you know, that particular cultural aspect does come in the recruitment procedure also. So what happens is that the recruitment procedure becomes very rigorous while in the case of the US, as we understand from what we know about doing business with the US and other English speaking countries, the recruitment processes and the procedures are low to medium actually. It's more on the need based. So if we talk about the need-based recruitment, if we talk about the Japanese style of working, even if the need is there, even if it is an urgent need, they will not know their different processes, and different steps of recruitment. They will keep it rigorous. And even if the position is left empty, they will not recruit a person till they are fully satisfied at the recruitment stage itself. If we talk of the fourth dimension of the management style of any country when we are comparing, we are talking about the level of employee training, the people who already are employed in the organizations.

What is the level of training provided by the company, the investment made in the employees by the company and the focus and the conviction that training is required, to what extent it is required. So in the case of Japanese companies, the Japanese style of working is a continuous process. Why is it continuous because Japanese people think the Japanese business people think that the employees whom they are likely to expect to work for a lifetime are the key success factors. So that is how they differentiate themselves from other companies by having good employees, well trained employees. So it is in the nature of Japanese companies to resort to and invest in the continuous training of its employees. While in the case of US companies, we find that the training process is as and when required. So US companies are not having continuous training. It is just the application of mind because one reason for that is that in the US companies generally the employees have individual freedom and they can easily be expected to leave the company whenever they find a better job somewhere else. So it really makes no business sense for the business people at the top level in the US companies to invest heavily in the continuous training of the employees. So obviously this difference does exist.

Comparing Japan And Us Management Styles - Part 2

Friends. If we talk of the fifth parameter of comparing the management style of Japan with the US. Let us talk about the worker's union. So what type of unions exist? What is the worker's protective environment or the things to protest or to complain about or go to some organization? In the case of becoming a victim of certain unexpected behavior by the employer. Worker's Union The job of a union is to look after the welfare of the workers, especially the blue-collar workers, shop floor workers. So in the Japanese system of management, generally expected workers unions are the single unions with which they have a kind of agreement, enterprise agreement.

Generally, the well-accepted fact is that each big company in Japan has the recognition of a single workers union, generally created by the companies themselves. And they are not really the independent workers union, which actually exists in the case of, for example, in the US and many other English-speaking countries in Europe. It is quite different. It is a kind of enterprise unionism. So this enterprise unionism exists in Japan which is quite different, but it works very well. You should not say that this is kind of a monopoly that has been created by Japanese companies to exploit the employees. That is not true, actually. Rather, the enterprise unions take the middle way, keeping the interest of the organization as well as the interest of the workers that work very well because if both are happy, the thing will work for a longer time.

It will be more sustainable, the relationship will be more cordial, and that is what actually is happening. But it is debatable whether this enterprise unionism is really the correct protection of the labor force. So a lot of debate takes place on this issue. There are a lot of researchers that are there on the union system in Japan that is quite different from many other advanced countries. If we talk about the workers' position and their status in the organization. So generally when we talk about the workers' status, we generally focus on the status of the blue-collar workers versus the white collar workers. So if we talk about the Japanese style of functioning, we see that the blue-collar workers and the white collar workers have single status. For all practical purposes, the status is single for the simple reason that by the management style of Japan, each white-collar worker has to start by becoming a blue-collar worker. So they have to spend time on the shop floor. They have to eat the same thing that other shopfloor workers eat. They have to be with them until they graduate into a white-collar job. The difference cannot exist. So the system is like that.

The difference between the blue-collar and the white-collar workers is not there in Japanese management style. It is a single status in the case of the US also, to a great extent, there is hardly any discrimination between the blue-collar workers and the white collar workers. But yes, their income levels are different and definitely, the differences exist. Although there is a lot of shortage today in US industries for blue-collar workers. So their status actually has gone up in the present time. If we talk of the seventh parameter on the understanding of the Japanese management style versus the US, we are talking of decision-making, how the decision-making takes place in the organizations, medium to large organizations in Japan versus how it is taken, and how it is done in the US. So in management jargon, we would say that the decision-making process in Japanese companies is bottoms-up which means generally the ideas and the suggestions start from the shop floor and a lot of importance is given to those kinds of suggestions and the ideas.

Generally, the top management people are very powerful people, but they do not involve themselves in the day-to -day activities. They only come into picture when it is really required and at the right time if some decision-making has to be done at their level. But generally, generally speaking, it is based on the bottoms-up approach and the things that are collected in a particular period of the ideas and sessions. In fact, they really work very fast on those ideas because, with time, the Japanese system has evolved and they have learned that it works very well, it improves the product features, it improves efficiency, it improves the output. If you hear from the bottom line at the shop floor, at the supervisor level, what are the difficulties they are facing? So it actually really helps for the company to create a strategic advantage vis a vis other companies.

So that is the learning which Japanese people already have and they are very proud of it. While in the case of US companies, generally speaking, the approach is normally tops down, although there is a lot of emphasis on individual freedom, people at all levels have the opportunity to speak up or to voice their complaints or even suggest and give ideas. And generally, the ideas are listened to, the concerns are listened to. in US companies. But finally, it is well accepted that the most powerful people at the top have their ideas and what they say their decision making prevails. Although the meaning of the top level in US companies is more to do with the profits and the shares and the compensation that the top person receives and the numbers and statistics he is able to generate for the companies. And generally, what happens, it is the individual preference of the top person in US companies, whether he wants a top-down approach and the bottom-up approach and generally what happens depends on the different types of industries and the nature of the business which the company is into.

In US companies, they choose between the bottom-up approach and the top-down approach or something, a trade off in between. So this is what we already know. I need not tell you about the management style of US companies. Most of the people who are in English speaking countries know the main features of the US management and working style.

Comparing Japan And Us Management Styles - Part 3

Now, friends, only a few of the other parameters we will discuss when we are talking about the differences in the management style of Japan and if we compare those things with the US companies, three parameters that are remaining that we will be talking about are the nature of the workers' groups. What kind of workers are there, the categories of the workers? I'm not talking about the blue color or white color. I'm talking about the permanent workers, the temporary workers or a mix of it. What actually are the methods of dealing with the workers, and how the labor is managed? So we are talking about labor laws. We are talking about so many things in this.

When we talk of the workers' groups and employee welfare and internal recruitment. So the workers ' group in Japan generally comprises the core workers who actually are expected to be working for their lifetime and the peripheral workers. So the peripheral workers' system has evolved in recent times in Japan. That is the not-so-permanent staff and depending on the need of the companies, they may be increased or decreased as the requirement and there is hire and fire in the peripheral workers' category. So there do exist these kinds of two categories that generally in the US companies it is not the case. So generally US companies do not work like that, at least in the US market itself, although US companies in other markets, overseas markets, do follow this system of core and peripheral two types of permanent and temporary workers groups. But in Japan it is very, very common.

Now if we talk of employee welfare, the type of welfare, the focus of the company is towards employees, what type of welfare we are talking about. So when we say the Japanese management style of providing the employees with the best of the working environment and the compensation and many other things. So I would say that basically, the focus of the Japanese companies is not on compensation, which is actually based on the seniority and the number of years somebody has worked in Japanese companies. But they do provide a complete package of welfare, which includes low-interest rate loans or cheaper housing facilities, the conveyance, free conveyance, free food in the companies, in many of the companies, they provide free lunch and many other facilities like medical facilities at almost no cost.

And the loan system interest-free or low-interest-rate loan system actually helps the Japanese companies to have a better control on the employees. So they treat it as a driving handle to be able to have better control, and a better grip on the employees. So it is very, very prevalent to provide the interest free or the low-interest loans to the employees when the need arises. And finally, when we are talking about the management style of Japan versus US, we are talking about another aspect of the management style, and that is the internal recruitment, which means if the vacancies exist at some certain higher levels. So it is a very, very common practice in Japan and it is very, very much prevalent that they recruit somebody internally from within the organization and that will become their first priority if they are not able to get somebody to fill that particular post. Only then do they go outside. So the focus and the first choice of the Japanese management style of working is for the Japanese companies to go for internal recruitment, while in the case of the US, it is purely based on the profile and the requirement of the job, the right match with the job.

And they definitely do not differentiate between the internal employees or somebody coming from other companies. So it purely depends on the HR people and the HR consultants that for what post, what profile is required, whether it will be filled internally or from outside. In many cases, it happens that the general consensus is that the particular post has to be filled by somebody from the third organization, an outsider. It is very, very common. So the management working style of Japan definitely is unique, but there is nothing to be alarmed with. That there is nothing really wrong with the Japanese management style of working. It is just that the understanding of the management style is very, very important to succeed in doing business with Japan.

Summary

So friends we studied leadership and management styles, and now we know that in this module we learned that local employees are certainly influenced by the local culture and have unconscious, out of consciousness in other words, preferences of the traits of an outstanding leader which is preferred by the local cultures. So what are the traits? What are the preferred traits, and implicit traits that an outstanding leader should have in those cultures? We have understood, and we have also understood that local influence does matter in forming those preferences. Therefore, the leader, when moving to other countries, has to learn and unlearn many personal habits, perceptions, and sometimes beliefs also, and sometimes even values also actually. But that's a little difficult area, but it has to be looked into to match with the expectations of the host culture. So it's a very, very complicated process that requires a high level of intercultural competence.

We finally studied about the Globe Project. That was a very large project which was undertaken by almost 200 researchers from 62 countries, and it took ten years to complete. So the Globe Project CLT dimensions, that means culturally endorsed implicit leadership theory dimensions, can help leaders in fine-tuning their leadership styles when dealing with different cultures and even multicultural workplaces, multicultural teams, and even multicultural remote teams. The leader-follower Interaction and exchange is a complex process of things like expectation, trust, emotions and the ethical values of the local culture. So these are some of the things that we had taken up in this module.

And finally, we also learned in this module the prevalent typical management styles and typical hierarchies that are significantly varying from country to country, even sometimes in the same region of the world. For example, within Europe, we have different countries with very different types of the typical management styles and different types of hierarchies that are present in their workplaces. So these are the things which we learnt in this module.

Overview

So, friends, do you know that 100 Israeli managers working in Silicon Valley in the US found that Israeli-American managers thought in more complex ways than managers who thought themselves to be belonging to only Israeli or only American cultures. The result was that the peers of these employees rated them as more competent managers and they were actually promoted faster. So these are the facts, actually. There are many, many such facts that are there which relate to cultural adaptation, intercultural existence of multicultural work teams and intercultural communication. So there are things definitely beyond just understanding the cultural differences, what we talked about in the last module. So these understandings in terms of leadership differences or management style differences are not sufficient.

We have to go beyond understanding those differences and look for ideas that explain very, very astonishing and incredible facts about the different cultures and the existence of people of Multi Cultures, the multicultural work teams. Do you think that cultural differences have an impact on the potential of business success for different national cultures? These are the questions that we are going to take up in this module. Questions like Can there be theoretical ideas that can help to design flexible organizations, flexible organization structures and management mechanisms in various forms of cultural atmospheres that are starkly different from each other? These are the things that we are going to take up in this particular module, and we will try to look at the different cross-cultural management theories in this module that goes definitely beyond the understanding of the differences in the management styles.

Introduction to CCM Theories

Now, friends, when we are talking about understanding the type of challenges that were there in the case study that we started with UNP, we have already understood certain models. So those models are not complete actually, there are many other models, but I chose only two models to explain to you the concept of cultural differences and cultural comparisons and to some extent the tips and techniques of cross-cultural management, but without understanding certain theories, certain ideas, getting the feel of the methods, what method should be used and in what situation. That kind of ability probably can only come through certain theories, and an understanding of the theories.

Now these are the ideas. These are the theories. You can say that to some extent these are the philosophies of life and the people and the cultures. But these theories actually are likely to help you in taking decisions with respect to the methods to be used for different cultures. Given the fact that most probably the cultural differences do not result in any poor performance or better performance, those things have got many other factors. It is not just because of the culture that some countries are rich and some countries are not rich, and whether being rich is a parameter of advancement is also debatable. So there are so many factors in this. Let us now start with a discussion on certain theories of cross-cultural management, of the culture, cultural differences and also cultural competence. So there is something called cultural competence.

This means the ability of certain cultures or certain people to be able to manage other cultures with the help of a very high level of cultural awareness. And that actually is also the purpose of this Book. One of the main purposes of this Book is to increase your cultural awareness that eventually, with your own efforts is likely to add to your cultural competence. So that is also one of the very important areas that you have to look into.

Jungle Theory of Cross Cultural Management

The first theory that I would discuss in cross-cultural management is the jungle theory of cross-cultural management. What do you think about why I am talking of the jungle, why I bring the jungle into this, and why I have chosen this, why I have chosen this as the first theory to discuss? It's a jungle theory because the jungle is a very natural ecosystem with the very diverse type of animals which are there in jungles and forests, and yet without any intervention from the humans, it works very well. It maintains the balance. The performance of jungles definitely is better than all the rest of the cities and the towns of the humans. So definitely the excellence of these jungles and forests that are managed by certain forces, the diverse types of animals and the success of the jungle and the forest because of the presence of so many animals and their diversity and their interdependence and their coexistence with each other are very remarkable. So I have chosen this theory.

I'm very sure that you will appreciate the fact that probably this idea of jungle and forest and the theory connected with this should help in cross-cultural management. So let us look at what actually is the theory about the jungle. What it says is that in the animal kingdom we know that there are very different and diverse types of animals. Each one is a winner in their own right and wants to live longer as they love what they are. So everybody is very happy with whatever faculties they have, whether it is Tiger, whether it is an elephant, and they have their own food habits, they have their own communication skills, the ecosystem, their way of living. All the animals have their own style and culture. You will notice that. So similarly diverse cultural traits do not represent losers and winners like in a jungle or in a forest.

Every diverse animal is a hero within their own species, which has survived thousands and probably millions of years of existence on earth without any major problems. Any living being that is there in the forest is a winner. So similarly, diverse cultural traits do not represent losers and winners. So it supports the fact, which I mentioned in my earlier chapter, that there is no bad culture or good culture. So you cannot compare and you cannot assume that a particular culture is backward or forward or bad or losing proposition or winning proposition. So you can't say that. So it is just that each culture requires an enabling environment to perform to the best of their capabilities and win the game. Like what happens in a jungle or in a forest. They get the right platform, and the right environment and they progress very well. So the same animals when you put them in zoos or in captivity, they get diseases. They do not perform the way they were supposed to in the wild. So they perform really well in the wild. In captivity it doesn't work.

So the same thing happens when we talk of cross-cultural management. So, for example, if we talk of the UNP case. In the UNP case, if the Upjohn managers knew that the Swedish and Italian companies would be better left to their ways of working and with minimum intervention, they should have got their job done. What was the benefit of the merger and acquisition, that is the pipeline, the product pipeline? They could have managed the R and D could have been managed if the Swedish and Italian cultures and their ways of working, the people from those nationalities would have been left to their ways of working. Upjohn would have done better by providing a better enabling environment, appreciation and celebration of diversity. So that is very, very important that they should have celebrated this diversity, these differences, in which case this jungle theory for a story would have helped in making all three entities, all the three geographical cultures, the winners, and the chances of the UNP becoming a success, and a high level of integration would have been very, very high.

So at the same time, diverse animals in a jungle are interdependent on each other in keeping the jungle ecology in check, healthy and in good balance. This theory was actually being debated in several conferences, but let me tell you, the ideas had already been mooted in certain conferences. This particular idea is likely to gain a lot of traction in businesses, if this method of jungle and forest theory is used in cross-cultural management, especially in the event of mergers and acquisition and many similar situation I think cross-cultural management will give very good results and the kind of fiasco that took place with the UNP that Upjohn, Pharmacia and Farmitalia, they all vanished from the market to become part of the Pfizer and the big fish ate away the smaller fishes in a market that now is more monopolistic in nature, which is not good for the industry as a whole. So this was this theory, the jungle theory of cross-cultural management, and probably you can read about it more, you can still find similar ideas in other research papers.

Role of Cultural Shock and Cultural Stress in building cultural competence

So, friends, what do you think? The UNP case. Did you notice certain kinds of shock and stress among the employees of Upjohn or the employees of Pharmacia? And perhaps the erstwhile employees of Farmitalia? In their own perspective, they were, I think, encountering their own type of shock and stress, and we call it the cultural shock and stress. This theory of cultural shock and stress is very, very important. And according to Kim 1988, cultural shock is not linearly and constantly adapting and changing phenomena, but a constant and cyclic one that, thanks to the intercultural stress, situations develop intercultural communication and adaptation skills through a constant development and learning process. So according to him, stress is treated as a positive phenomenon with respect to the adaptation process. But Of course, shock can result in certain fiascos of the types that took place in UNP.

In all probability, the reaction of Upjohn was the result of the cultural shock. Cultural stress is still acceptable because cultural stress makes you learn new things, makes you learn new methods of dealing with the situation, but it definitely does not add to the big cost of what really happened with UNP or the reduction in profits. What actually happened? If the formula was good, the cultural stress would have helped Upjohn to rethink the strategy, celebrate the diversity and they would have done the right things to make sure that the outcome and the results brought about by Pharmacia and Farmitalia employees are as desired and as required by the market. After all, the merger was in the mutual interest of both entities. So this theory talks about the intensity of the cultural shock that is very high and can lead to the wrong decisions of the managers of the type what happened with

Upjohn managers, while cultural stress is not that intense, it gives room for rethinking in some ways hiding the feelings.

So if you do not understand a particular culture, you are going through stress and you really don't feel good about a particular culture. So instead of having cultural shock, if you can reduce it to cultural stress, you will be able to find ways of dealing with that and not making sure that there is any adverse impact on your company or your entity. So that is the idea about this.

Theory Of Comfort Of Local Cultures With Foreign Cultures In Mnes

Now friends. There is another cultural theory on which I have actually worked a lot. So when I talk about cross-cultural management, we are talking about multicultural workplaces in multinational companies or companies dealing with international operations. When we are talking of multicultural workplaces, there are people of different nationalities in particular groups with their own belief system and they are in a way different animals in the jungle and they have their own habits, food habits, their own perspective in their own right. So what happens?

Certain nationalities, background people are more comfortable with certain nationalities of colleagues with certain national backgrounds, than some other colleagues with another third national origin. So the level of comfort between two pairs of workers in the same team with different cultural backgrounds can vary from one pair to another depending on the interaction of the two persons in the pair with different types of cultural backgrounds and beliefs. According to the research paper that was actually submitted by me only along with Professor Rahul Singh of BIMTECH in 2013, I started work on this research and I did a study on the level of comfort between employees of local and foreign cultures in multinational firms. So the result of this study indicated that if you know which combinations of cultural pairs, cultural background pairs in multicultural workplaces have more comfort or less comfort and the reasons for those differences.

And if you find some methods to deal with those situations and some restructuring of the teams in such a way that the level of comfort gaps is not very, very high, it is possible to manage the situation in a better way. So, for example, if I give you one example when I say in the UNP case the three cultures that were involved were America, Sweden and

Italy. Now Italian culture is Indo-European culture, Swedish culture is Scandinavian culture, a more feminine type of culture, while US culture is more masculine in nature. So if you find the level of comfort between these three types of cultures, you will find that in all probability, the cultural comfort between Italians and Swedish would be better when compared to the combinations involving the Swedish versus US and Italian versus US. So these studies can be done by using the Hofstede model also.

And you can also look at this research paper and you can find out the cultural comfort scores of different countries like Hofstede scores, and you will get an idea of which countries are culturally near and which countries are culturally distant. These kinds of studies can help you in managing the cross-cultural environment and multicultural workplaces in international operations. So what do you think? If you think from your own imagination, if your colleague is with someone from the African continent or if you have some colleagues with a European culture or a US culture in your country, they are working. So do you see the possibility of your nearness or less comfort or more comfort with a particular person of a particular origin? Do you really see? So do some kind of exercise and try to find out if you have that situation. If you are working in any multicultural workplace, try to find out. Do you see those differences? Do you really feel that there are certain differences in the level of comfort of the local culture with the foreign cultures in the business, in the workplaces?

Stages of Cultural Adaptation

A similar theory that adds to and complements the theories that have just been discussed deals with the cultural adaptation that I talked about when I was talking about cultural shock and cultural stress. What do you think about the cultural adaptation of different cultures in multicultural workplaces or multicultural situations like UNP? What do you see that the adaptation would be of a particular pattern or will be smooth or it will be constant? What is your opinion about the shape of the cultural adaptation of one culture with another culture, a particular culture with another particular culture?

As per the theory and the research done by James Rajshekhar and Frank Renad in 2013 and this research paper, you can find out on the Net. What they found is that cultural adaptation has got stages, certain stages. Definitely the time frame may vary from situation to situation, country to country, but the stages more or less match in the cultural adaptation with any types of particular pairs of the cultural interaction. So depending on which culture with which culture is being compared or adapted. For example, in the UNP case, when we talk of the American culture with Sweden or the American culture with Italian, what will be the stages of adaptation? The type of stages may be the same, but the time frame may vary. It may be a little easier to reach the mature stage in the adaptation process with Sweden probably, and it may take a longer time for Italian adaptation to American culture. So these differences will remain, but these stages will be very similar, as has been observed by many, many experts. So as per this theory, stages of cultural adaptation start with phase one. That is the pre-departure ups and downs.

This means, for example, if we take the example of Upjohn managers, some of them being deputed to Sweden to oversee the operations there, pre-departure, there will be a lot of misconception about the new culture and certain jitters, ups and downs. And at the stage when the person is moving to a different culture, being exposed to an absolutely different culture to see it in reality, there will be a certain amount of honeymoon period when his emotional being will be at a very, very healthy level, emotional level. And with time, certain times, it may get converted into some level of culture shock or cultural stress coupled with the acute homesickness. So depending on the time frame for how long the assignment of the person is in a new culture, the possibility of homesickness would be more because of the longing of the person of a similar lifestyle that he has enjoyed for many, many years in the home culture. That person misses those kinds of moments, and that leads to homesickness and the distance between the person from the dear ones also add to that situation. But after a certain time of the shock and stress of the cultural dimensions, the person tends to adapt to the new culture.

This is a very good phase because this phase has to be a little longer so as to successfully complete the assignment that he is doing in the new culture, in the destination culture. And again, when the time comes to return back to the home culture, similar pre-departure ups and downs again comes so pre-return ups and downs again set in for the person, but with the experience. So the person has now the adapted experience he has experienced during the honeymoon period. He has also experienced cultural shock along with homesickness which he has been able to cope with after a certain time. So with this experience and a new type of ups and downs, he again comes back to the home culture with certain excitement on returning to the home culture. And after some time, this excitement again dips to the poor emotional well-being associated with missing the good elements and good moments of the new culture that he was exposed to. So with this experience and the two stages of ups and downs, the honeymoon phase and Excitement phase finally, the person became very much adapted and very confident in being able to deal with a new culture if given another chance and the person now is more culturally aware. He is now more culturally competent.

What is the meaning of this? That this particular theory gives a very good idea of the methods of creating cultural awareness and cultural competence among the employees. So in the case of UNP, UpJohn managers should have been sent on a cyclic basis for anything between 1 to 3 months or four months assignments immediately after the merger, so that they would have passed through these stages and would have come out well adapted with strong cultural competence and cultural awareness. If that number of managers would have increased and they would have been put in the key position to manage the Pharmacia operations in Sweden and already acquired Farmitalia Italian employees groups, those people would have done very good cross-cultural management. So the parent company needs to regularly send its managers for short and medium-term duration assignments to subsidiaries abroad. So this is the inference that we can get from this theory. And this is also the chapter that is the cross-cultural chapter that we get from this theory.

Role of Cognitive Diversity in Organizational Performance

Then friends. Very popular, very interesting theory of Horwitz, S.K. and Horwitz, I.B. that was mooted in 2007 that propagates the idea that cognitive diversity actually is good. So if we relate this theory with the fact that in jungle and forest theory, the animals of different types definitely give better results for the overall balance and the functioning of the ecosystem of forest. If certain species are out of the forest, it may lead to major damage to the forest environment. For example, in many of the forests and jungles in India, where the tiger population was reduced to zero, the degradation of the whole ecosystem started. And it is a proven fact.

The same thing happens when this theory propagates that cognitive diversity among humans helps build a better environment for better performance in the businesses. Because many researchers, as per this theory, contend that the physical diversity characteristics such as different races, different ages, different sex, and gender differences, also known as the bio demographic diversity, positively influences the performance of the companies because team members contribute unique cognitive attributes based on their experiences stemming from their demographic background. So one example I will like to give you for supporting this particular theory.

You will notice that the multinational companies from Japan, a handful of them, are really very successful in electronics and automobiles, but many, in fact the majority of the multinational companies originating from Japan are failures in international business because of the ethnocentric approach and the monogamous culture in those companies. That means the Japanese culture that is unique in its own right they have been not able to bring in the outsiders, the other cultures within the ambit of the work

environment in those companies, and they could not succeed internationally. So companies like Sony, companies like Mitsubishi, companies like Toyota, and Suzuki, have partially or fully succeeded in having very, very successful, very excellent international companies. But those companies' numbers are limited when compared with other countries from Western Europe and the USA. Fortune 500 companies list if you look at you will find the number of Japanese companies much less than in many other countries. So the reason is very simple.

The major failure of Japanese companies has been not appreciating cultural diversity in the recruitment process and the maintenance of human talent in those companies. So such failures have really badly hit many of the excellent companies from Japan. So many observations actually support this particular theory, and it has a lot of traction in international business, including in mergers and acquisition. And it also indicates if we apply these same theories on the UNP case, actually speaking, if Upjohn had been able to manage the Pharmacia, the Swedish group as well as the Italian group, the Upjohn managers would have been very, very sure that the overall performance would have been actually very good if the cross-cultural management would have been done in the proper manner, with a proper understanding and with proper cultural competence and cultural awareness. If Upjohn managers would have been trained in this area well in advance before going into the merger and acquisition, this theory would have ensured that the overall performance of the UNP, the merged entity, the fully and properly integrated, culturally integrated UNP, would have performed much better in the market.

Conclusion

So, friends, we had a very interesting module and we found that in this module that definitely there is nothing called bad or good cultures. People from all national cultures can give outstanding performances given the right opportunity and work environment and leadership. We also learned in this module that cross-cultural shocks and stresses can prove to be a great cross-cultural teacher and have the potential to increase cross-cultural competency. That is very, very important in today's world of transnationals, which depend on the team of managers with very high quality of cross-cultural competence. And we also learned in this module that the process of cross-cultural adaptation is a set of stages involving several ups and downs, periods of highs and lows of emotional well-being, stable stages of adaptation in between.

And those are the real focus to get the benefit of the cultural adaptation that actually benefits the organization. So those are the things to focus on. Those are the periods, the stable periods of adaptation that are in between or later after the encounter. So these things we studied in this module friends, and then we also learned in this module that having multicultural work teams can increase the chances of business success. That is a great learning we had and we will be talking about it more in this Book. And then finally, we now know that the level of comfort between managers from different cultures and different cultural backgrounds may vary according to the specific cultures to which they belong to or they come from. So there are many permutations and combinations of people with dual cultures or single cultures or high levels of acculturation. This whole area is very complex, but with the type of understanding that we have done through the cross-cultural models studied in this module, things become easy and it helps in taking good decisions, good business decisions.

Creating a Happy Marriage and Loving Relationship

Do you often feel pressured when you think about approaching an attractive looking girl in public or even in a one on one situation, do you brush off the entire idea with thoughts that end up demeaning you as not being good enough or for the fear that the entire thing would end up in an awkward or hurtful manner? Do you often feel just too shy to do anything about it and end up regretting your decision and what to do and what not to do when you approach her and how to stay in touch with her? If you've answered yes to any one of these questions and you've come to the right Book, that will guarantee an improvement in your first impressions and self-confidence game.

Welcome to a First Timers Guide to Approach Girls, the basic dos and don'ts. We'll be working on your self-confidence, building the game plan when going in some basic gentlemen roles as in how to behave, what things to talk about and so forth. And we hope that by the end of this Book, you'll have a more realistic outlook of reading situations, realizing your own self-worth and overcoming this rooted fear that will enable you to see that there's absolutely nothing to be fearful or nervous about when dealing with a girl for the first time. Now onto the Book, it'll be divided into three segments before, during and after, signifying the three stages that you'll go through of the entire process. There are also some miscellaneous chapters specifically dedicated to where most of the issues arise in these situations.

You won't have to worry about prerequisites. There are no prerequisites here. The only one you'll need is the desire and the will to change your current situation. And with enough time, practice and learning, we're sure you'll stand out from the rest when it comes to introducing yourself, being friends with or when making a first impression with a female. And we surely hope you'll see the Book paying off for you. As always, when it comes to these online chapters, communication with your instructor is the key to getting the most out of it.

Be sure to drop any relevant or legitimate questions you feel might need to be answered, and we'll try getting back to you as soon as possible. Since there are many people who take these Books. Getting through all the questions takes time, but we make sure every query gets answered. Do share this Book with your friends. If you find it helpful, that would give us a better sense. If we're doing good will appreciate you pointing out any confusion you come across and we'll fix that as well. So go ahead and enroll yourself and we'll see you in the next chapter.

Overview

We really appreciate you enrolling and we really thank you for it and welcome you and join us on this journey of stepping out of your comfort zone and jumping right into the game. Now it's on our part to make sure you've made the right choice of enrolling with us. We hope to deliver you the very best that will enable you to step up for yourself. Let's get started with the Book overview. Now, the chapters you will present here will be between three to five minutes. Some important chapters may extend beyond that.

The reason they might come across as short is that the chapters are to the point and not like those 19 minute chapters that just waste the first 15 minutes saying vague stuff in the 16th with some very obvious advice and everything after that beginning to sign up for their websites or to buy their books. We value your time and money and we want to help you reach your goal. Having said that, we'll start by going over the topics of the lessons. Episode one introduction. This is a beginner's guide to the purpose, aims, objectives and expected outcomes of this Book to overview a look at what our outline is. That's what we're doing right now. Three Before you get started, some basic pointers to know before going out there for miscellaneous tips on confidence boosting.

We'll get down towards some essential ways you can boost your confidence. Game five approaching. We'll look at some different situations and read the atmosphere before deciding on an appropriate approach. Six initiating conversation ways on how to get her attention and setting the grounds on starting a progressive conversation. Seven ways to not be nervous. There will be moments during your conversation, Will. You'll start to panic. This chapter will help you stay in check with yourself and what to talk about. Now that you have her attention, you'd want to have a conversation that's both interesting and meaningful to the both of you. Nine What not to talk about. Guys always bring up topics that most girls are just too uncomfortable talking about or would leave a bad first impression. Then how to keep her interested.

Now that you have her attention, you'll need some basic ideas on what and how exactly you need to do things in order to keep the conversation smooth and engaging in getting her number. You're about to part ways, but you want to stay in touch. Getting her number is the most crucial part to ever seeing her again. Twelve reaching out on social media, Snapchat adding girls you never met before or ones you just met. Thirteen reaching out on social media Instagram following the lead of the previous chapter, this election stayed specific to Instagram. Fourteen texting the basic rules of how, when and what to text about. Fifteen Miscellaneous How to flirt during a text conversation. Do you find yourself attracted to her and feel the feeling might be mutual? Find out what to do in this chapter. Sixteen Carrying on how to handle relationships. You are free to study at your own pace. We'd recommend you going one chapter at a time with at least a day's break in between. But really it's up to you.

You can always come back and revisit chapters and like mentioned in the previous chapter, feel free to ask any question related to the chapter and we will be sure to get back to you due to the fact that we are serving several thousands of students at a time. Our responses may vary in time, but we'll be sure to get yours in due time. The chapters prepared are short, concise, yet extremely relevant and to the point which will make sure you aren't wasting your time. The websites will ask you for review, which you may feel however you found the chapter. But a positive review is what drives us knowing we're actually making a difference in your lives. Nothing pleases us more and we promise you the utmost level of dedication and commitment.

The next chapter is where we formally begin with our content. We would recommend you grabbing a small notebook just to jot down an important point or question you may be relevant. Our doors are always up for discussion as well. Having said that, see you in the next chapter. And once again, thank you for entrusting us with this.

chapter three before getting started. Picture this, you finally decided on stepping up for yourself and are on the verge of making that approach. When you start doubting yourself and question yourself whether you look good enough or not, your friends are the popular guys, you know, might come across saying things like looks don't matter. But that's usually advice you'll get from people who've been good looking all their lives and don't really realize the importance of what they've had.

It's like the equivalent of a rich guy telling you money can't buy happiness. Heck, they might as well just give it over to you then, but won't see the analogy. The thing about looks is that they do matter, but they don't really matter that much. If you're an average looking guy with an average personality in a girl's eye, you're average at best. If you're an average looking guy with a great personality, you're likely about a seven out of 10. And that's decent enough. It's important to realize that these factors both go hand in hand and average out for an overall first impression. Having good looks isn't really a necessity, but dressing sharp will definitely boost your chances of coming across a potential candidate to have a conversation with. So the first step is for you to forget that you're not looking good enough. Heck, I've seen some really fat guys land. Not even kidding.

You should think to yourself if an average looking guy or even a below average looking guy can do it, they might be doing something right. And looks definitely aren't such a big factor. Realizing and convincing yourself is one of the most difficult things of the Book. But over time you'll be sure to convince yourself, since not looking good can be scratched off the list. Realize that you can compensate for it by dressing up good or just seeming interesting. Hopefully we won't have to explain the difference here. First of all, let's get the obvious out of the way, which includes grooming a proper hairstyle, not dressing immaturely and smiling. So we're not going to waste time talking about that because it's so obvious that anyone with a little common sense can come up with that stuff. And all that is available practically everywhere you look.

This chapter isn't going to be one of those generic ones, but would instead focus on the more specific factors in your control right now. The first and foremost thing is to be positive, there's nothing more annoying than a guy who's constantly nagging or doesn't seem like he's in a good mood. Being positive just brings out a vibe that allows other people to be around you more often. Don't believe me. Take a look around yourself and look for what all the positive people around you have in common. It'll probably be that a lot of people like being around them. Positivity also feels good. Think about it. Positive people are active and enjoy doing the things they do. They smile a lot and nothing gives out a warm welcome. More than that, an important point worth noting is that it doesn't mean you should pretend to have fun or fake your way through. That will only give out the impression that you're just trying to have fun.

Not only does that give out a creepy, weird vibe, but it also makes you uncomfortable. And what you're doing, enjoy what you do. If you find yourself in a situation that's not entirely your thing, the least you can do is try to find something interesting in it. For example, if parties aren't your thing but you find yourself at one anyway, you can always meet people. Be around the DJ. If you're into meeting new people or music, there's always something to look for. Try it. The next thing that'll up your level is you actually having some interest, it's essential for you to have a hobby, a dream or something you're deeply passionate about. Let's face it, meeting a girl with absolutely no life, ambition or passion, it all comes across as unattractive. Think about it. The same can be said in a reverse role. Have any kind of passion just so long as you deeply care about it. Cars, the environment, the latest new hit TV series, Anything will do. The last thing we're going to discuss is how much to talk, don't be the kind of person who's too shy to say a word that people end up unconsciously ignoring or that person who talks too much that it just straight up becomes annoying.

Find the perfect balance in between and work on it. Try reading the nature of the conversation you might be interested in and contribute to it accordingly. The last thing left is being confident, but that's a trait we'll cover in the next election with great detail because it's one of the most important aspects when it comes to improving yourself. As of this chapter, realize that there are certain checkboxes that determine you as an overall lacking in one doesn't mean that the overall can't be made up for looks and personality. Are the two checkboxes covered here? Dress up well and have a hairstyle that suits you to look good? Try growing a beard to see if that works for you. These are things that you can find with a simple Google search. Personality should have a bit more priority. Be confident and positive, have a hobby and passion you deeply care about and try to have fun even in the little things without overselling it. That should be it for this chapter. Feel free to ask any questions and we'll see you next time.

chapter for being confident. So you finally took that first step toward approaching girls, but there's this constant feeling of nervousness that makes you doubt what you're doing. It's totally natural to feel that, in fact, it's one of the most problems I'm often asked about. Getting nervous and overcoming self-doubt isn't hard at all. And after some time and self effort, you'll see yourself rising past it and feeling a huge boost in the way you see yourself as a person.

And all of this can also play a massive role in a girl actually liking you when you approach. So it's absolutely essential that you make the most of it. Let's get started. The first and most basic thing to do is self realization, identify your shyness and take steps towards reducing it, understand your behavior when you're put under situations where you feel shy. Do you not talk at all? Do you mumble when you talk or do you speak too much out of sheer nervousness? Understand and accept the fact that everyone feels shy in their certain situations. Most people just do a better job of hiding it than others.

Realizing your certain situation and your behavior can be a massive step towards resolving it. The next step you'd want to do is to force a different perspective about yourself. Tell yourself you're going to give 100 percent in what you do today. Tell yourself you're awesome. Believe in yourself. This may sound cheesy, but I'd seriously recommend you try to do it paired with the things that I'll suggest later on in this chapter. Believe in yourself and don't get distracted with what people say about you. What matters is your close friends' opinions because they're usually honest and straightforward. Other people will just have a one line judgment without anything solid to base it on. Psychology study has shown that we are very prone to our peers' comments and opinions. Take the example of Brexit or Trump's election. Even though people knew they were controversial stances, they ended up going with it simply due to an overwhelming majority opinion. It's essential that you defy this.

Do not listen to the people who try to bring you down. Now, onwards to things that you should do to boost your game. The first thing for you to do is start working out and exercising. This will not only make you look good, but feel good about yourself to start eating healthy, too, because that'll make you feel better about yourself. Don't just jump right into that, though. You can start small and gradually work your way to a balanced diet. This will also help you with getting into shape and will be good for things like your skin and complexion too. Like discussed in the previous chapters, getting a hobby not only gets you a better chance of talking to her, but at the same time knowing something you know you're good at can be a massive boost in your self-confidence.

Read up on the things that interest you and talk about it. It is sports, tech or even physics. It could be anything just as long as you know how to bring it up and talk about it in an interesting way. And we'll get to that. Similarly, dressing well is important, too, when you walk into a room knowing that you're the most well dressed person in there who can play a massive role in how you see yourself, even if you're not the most handsome guy in the room, you'll even get a handful of girls checking you out. And that's something none of us would have a problem with. Never make a decision based on other people's opinion. Do what you want and be yourself. Don't be embarrassed if you're into nerdy things or if you like unpopular opinions. An example is that I've been a Nickelback fan for a long time and have had to endure people making fun of me for that. But I never changed my taste on what people think because only I know what I like.

Being yourself and doing what you like makes you confident. Everyone later accepted me for my unpopular taste in music and I didn't have to change for anyone or lose my confidence. Win. Win. Right. Step five, make friends. It's easy to make friends even at this point of your life, the only basic and simple rule to follow is to not be creepy, and you're good to go get to know people different from you. Get in touch with a jock or a nerd, find common ground, something the two of you have a mutual interest in, bond over it. It can be fun, helpful and even uplifting. You don't have to be the best of friends, but keeping a good relationship with different people will always make you feel more likable and adaptable.

Do keep in mind to surround yourself with positive people. Only having negative people in your life can be a huge risk and might just blow up in your face. No pressure, no six have goals. Spend your time well. Try to do things that are both meaningful to you and productive at the same time. Let's think about this being an Internet troll who does nothing but sits on Reddit or YouTube all day long in wages. Common words. Girls don't find that attractive. I don't find that attractive. Nobody finds that attractive, find meaningful work for yourself, do what you like and don't care what people think about it. Which coincidentally pairs up with not getting offended by little things and spending time debating about it. That only gives the vibe that you have nothing going on in your life and that's never turns on. Instead, quite the opposite.

Have goals you legitimately want to pursue and work towards them. That will give you self-satisfaction and a better control over your life and finally set standards for yourself. Never settle for less than what you think you deserve. Learn to speak up for yourself and always push for the better. That will give a more dominant impression on girls like that. To sum up, believe in yourself. Move towards a healthy lifestyle. Don't be embarrassed about what things you're into. Get hobbies, dress presentable at all times. Adopt a positive outlook by surrounding yourself with positive people and be approachable and finally never settle for less than what you realistically think you deserve. These are things to surely boost up your confidence game, which will really play an important part in the long term until the next chapter. Thank you.

Approaching

chapter five approaching now that you've got some things to be confident about and you feel like you're ready to jump right in, you'd want to know the perfect way in approaching her. Don't be surprised if you find yourself in that spot. Not knowing how to do it is one of the leading causes for awesome guys like you not getting to know some potentially great girls out there. We've learned steps to being confident in these chapters about putting those steps in action. Consider yourself at a party where you see this pretty looking girl to the side of the room by yourself. You know, you have the perfect opportunity to go make an impression. What do you do? Most of you would back away and decline. What could be something good for you, either because you're still not that confident enough or you're confused on what exactly to do. If it's the former, you should go back to the previous chapter and revise and actually do the building up on the confidence part. If it's the latter, then we're about to dive right into it.

The most important part is to show you're confident and totally self-sufficient when approaching her. First of all, try reading her. Is she taking a break from all the fun she probably had or is she by herself unhappy? Make your approach accordingly. If the former makes your presence known so that she does notice, you talk to people, have some fun and try establishing that likable guy presence. I know that's easier said than done, but if the opportunity like that comes, don't let it go to waste. It could be your make or break moment. So definitely take notice of you and might even give you a look. That's a good sign. If you seem like she's in a bad mood, chances are she might not like where she is in both cases.

Keep in mind or in every situation, your approach should be positive, be confident and speak up. When you do say something, we'll get to that when you try to approach her by being confident. I mean, let it show. Do not be hesitant. Girls are extremely good at detecting body language and can tell if you're being fake. Ease yourself, relax and keep calm. This is one of the fundamentals in approaching. When you go on to start a conversation again, we will get to that. Say what you're going to say confidently. Girls find that attractive. The game is not about what you say. It's more along the lines of how you say it. A guy mumbling, slouching and stuttering versus a guy who's clear, upright and confident will have no chance by a landslide margin, even if both of them say the exact same thing. Like I said, it's all in body language. And having a confident one will definitely make the odds work in your favor.

The next step is to do all that I've told you with a smile on your face. It mostly comes down to what kind of situation you read. It'll be a good idea to do so, like about 95 percent of the time. Reading the situation should be easy. Like don't approach and smile at funerals. Obviously, a smile gives off the vibe that you have positivity in your life. And like already mentioned before, it attracts people. A smile paired with everything mentioned before makes for a huge chance in her not brushing you off as a creep and would make her feel more open to engaging in a conversation with you now for the hesitation you feel before going in and worrying what to talk about, I'm going to give you a tip that's going to work in nearly every situation. Say whatever you feel like saying.

Think about it and try to remember the very first thing you said to your best friend. When you approach them or when they approach you, you don't remember. Right, because it doesn't matter. People don't remember what you say. Just so long as it's not offensive or absurd, it could be any random topic on the condition that you're saying it in a confident manner, because impressions are what matter most in situations like these. And this works for every scenario, like in the park, on the street or in a waiting room. The next chapter is going to address this in a bit more detail. But for the time being, it's a good idea to go over the information I've already provided you in this

chapter. As always, you can post any questions and I'll be sure to get back to you until next time.

Initiating Conversations

chapter six, initiating conversations now that you've got our attention, it'd be wise to actually say something and not come across as a creep. You remember the saying that a girl usually takes eight minutes to decide if she actually likes you or not? Well, it's true and crucial for you to make those eight minutes count. The best way to initiate a conversation is that you talk about something that'll get her to talk to you as well. Don't stick to cheesy pickup lines. Those never work out at all that much and taking risks with them just aren't worth it.

Simplicity is key to this can start by something you've observed being around you, something that she's doing or any subject worth talking over. Just very simple things, really. Don't overdo it by straight up talking about her looks. There's a good chance she'll reject you immediately like all the other guys she's probably done. It's important that you don't make her feel objectified. Instead, bring up something like the party. You guys are at a simple line like, man, I really enjoy a good party. After a week's worth of work and right after a good workout, this line helps her to know a little bit about you and might prompt engagement. This would establish the impression that you have your life together, a routine and that you work out. All these odds can shift in your favor with just one simple, honest and straightforward line. Easy, right?

Moreover, you can craft any combination of lines just so long as they're meaningful and not creepy. And you should be good to go. Anything random and confident will work in your favor and establish you as a likable guy. The next thing to keep in mind is that you're trying to have a conversation, basically to have her talking as well. You can get this going for you by prompting her for her opinion. It's a good idea that you open up first, have a small story, not just points, but the emotion behind what you say and why you say it, because that acts as the basis for her to actually get to know you better without wasting time. Remember, we're in an eight minute time limit where every second counts. Do bring out the Y in what you do. That gives a huge chance with her feeling relatable to your situation.

All this so far would work so much better than a pick up line or simply standing there awkwardly having opened up. It's the perfect time to engage her in the conversation. Now, a simple question in continuation would do just fine in continuing our previous example, ending your introduction with a question like So what brings you to this party would definitely get her to talk to you. And that's pretty much it. You've successfully initiated a conversation with a girl. The important things to remember here are that you be presentable, confident and clear while having a hint of emotion behind all that. That's the essential part in starting conversations because it helps them better connect with you on a mental level and they really can't get enough of that.

Another example could be a girl at a coffee shop, you could say something like, I know it's a little silly, but I really can't get started with my day if I don't have that coffee. It's not your coffee name paired with today's paper before going into work every Tuesday. It's one of my favorite things to do here. See, it gives emotion, a back story and a good and meaningful vibe from you. You can land it by concluding with a question like how come you've not seen her here before, her coffee choice or her Tuesday morning ritual or anything like that. And introduce yourself. You should be good to go. And it works really easily. Homework goes out tonight to approach at least five different girls a day and make some small conversations with them. You'll instantly see the difference these chapters are making. Don't give out excuses like you don't know how to start conversations because now you do get that conversation. Practice working until next time.

Ways Not To Be Nervous

chapter seven ways not to be nervous by now, you're probably on cloud nine and feel like you're on fire because you just single handedly started something you never thought you would do. But here you are actually talking to a girl. It's all good until you realize something like, I've got this girl's attention. Now, this one scary thought happens to even the best of us at times. And we end up choking on a perfectly good opportunity. This chapter addresses just that. Once you start to get nervous, you give out plenty of signs that are red flags that are as clear as day, your heart just might start pounding too much. You might turn red and eventually come to an awkward halt and just stand there. These signs can be read by the girl you'll be talking to and might make her uncomfortable to the extent that she'll be ready to ignore and move on from you at any second. Just waiting for that chance. Here's some tips to fix that. No. One, stay comfortable, be in an atmosphere you're comfortable in. This cannot be the solution every time since you never know where you're going to meet that one person. But if you do want to make a move on her, this is one tip that can greatly work to your advantage. But your favorite place around your friends or your favorite time of the day, this will help you think of things to talk about and stay calm and cool.

The second one may be a bit hard for some people, but it's one of the most effective methods to adopt the method that states that no matter what or under any circumstances, you must convince yourself that you're not going to pursue her, even if you basically intend to. This is one of those methods that will put a lot of pressure off of you through this. You can feel a whole lot at ease. You'll probably not stutter and it'll be just like talking to a guy or an average person. There will be no one ending tension in the air and that'll work to your advantage. I've mentioned before that girls are really good at detecting body language.

Having someone who gives off the vibe that he really, really wants to pursue her, makes her want to talk to him less or not at all. It's more of a human thing.

We all take for granted the things that come easily to us. Having those signs crystal clear would make you come across as a creep. And that's not what you want. Convince yourself that you're not pursuing her. Instead, you're getting to know someone and just talk to spend some time together. Don't feel pressured that you'd want to see her again or that you'll have to get her. No, just take it easy. The next thing you'd want is to maintain your image in front of her. Don't be the guy who was all confident in approaching her at first but got flat when she actually started talking. Visualize yourself as the confident, social, likable guy you've been practicing to be. Keep that in mind before approaching her. And you should be all right. It's always good to get yourself in a good mood before going in, read up on some funny jokes or short stories, try nine gags or read it. That'll help you get in a good mood and it will add to your positive vibe. And if you find yourself in awkward silence with her, it'll be good to bring it up.

Unless it's offensive, sexist or racist, you should be good. The next step is to visualize what she'll say, how you'll say what you say and what kind of emotional vibe you'll be giving out when you do so. Mentally preparing yourself ahead of time is a good idea. Just be sure not to overcomplicate things. Remember to not overthink in situations like these. Just do enough for yourself that you don't see yourself stuck. The next step is not to panic when you're with her and when you start to get nervous the more you fight it, the more nervous you'll be and the more nervous you'll be, the more it'll become apparent. The best thing to do is to accept power through it, pretend like the feeling isn't there. There's something that'll come with practice. So do go around meeting people enough that you can learn to overcome this feeling, use all of the things mentioned as a learning experience of sorts as well. So the next time you do actually get nervous, you're more prepared for it if you're inexperienced.

See if you can try some way to work out what's the best way to handle things and what are the pointers worth taking from those experiences. You can also use the experiences to read body language, to read what she's thinking, and that will work for you as well. And the last one, act as who you want to be. You already have some goals for yourself and maybe you haven't pursued all of them just yet. Whether it's becoming a millionaire athlete or very successful businessman, act as if you were the most successful version of you from the future. In the future, you will be nervous when talking to a techno girl. Visualize yourself as that and you should be good to go. Do go over these tips again and try putting them in motion. In the next few days, you'll be better able to adapt to different situations and you'll learn to handle them in the smoothest possible way. I hope this chapter has been of some use to you guys. See you all next time.

What to Talk About

chapter eight, what to talk about before going in, there are some things you should go over just to keep things smooth or avoid any awkward situations. This chapter will focus more towards what are the key things to have in your conversation. The actual material will come in the chapter to keep her interested. Since both of these chapters overlap quite heavily, I found it better to include it in that one for better understanding and the maximum use. One great way of knowing what to talk about can be to prepare things you're going to talk about beforehand.

Observer before going in, try to pick out anything interesting about her. Does her laptop or mobile cover refer to a movie or music after she's into it? Or does her T-shirt have the name of a famous band like Nirvana on it or anything at this point? Really, if that doesn't work out and you're unable to deduce anything you can get out of observation is fine. Don't make it weird by constantly staring at her. It's creepy and they can sense it somehow. When you do go up to her and introduce yourself, like mentioned previously, you can talk about anything just so as long as it is interesting to the both of you and you're confident about it, you can talk about your surroundings, your life, the things that inspire you, anything where she'll show signs of being interested in what you have to offer. One way of knowing that she's actually listening to you, she'll have her body facing you or she'll even ask questions or seem interested.

Don't hesitate over this too much. If you've picked up on the previous chapters, well, know that you've got this. The next thing to do is ask her questions, try to ask her questions that will bring off emotional responses. Again, I can't stress how important it is to do this because most girls find emotional conversations, addicting and plain question and answer sessions about the why part extremely boring. Plus, you really don't get to know the person asking is also important because it establishes the basis and stays true to the definition of conversation. It's totally pointless if you're the only one talking. The final thing you can talk about are questions that you came prepared with, questions like if you could change any one thing in the world, what would it be? Or questions like who's one person dead or alive you'd ask out to dinner if given the chance and why the latter one might be a generic one now, but hopefully you get the idea questions that not only trigger emotional responses, but also get them to open up about themselves.

This helps you carry on the conversation, keep her interested and gives you time to think. If she's worth the effort, you'll know if you get some incredibly dumb answers that this girl isn't worth the effort of going out with later or being friends with, for that matter. Remember, have standards. This chapter has been a short one purely for the basis that you realize a couple of game changing aspects of approaching. The first, you can talk about anything just so long as you're confident, passionate about it and not a total creep or offensive. The conversation should be of interest to the both of you. And if you feel like it's not, you can always subtly change the topic with a question.

The second thing to remember is that you're looking for emotional responses. Remember, opening up yourself gets her to open up about herself. And that's the key for establishing a good conversation. Take the time to reflect on this chapter and preferably go out and talk to someone new and apply this method on people practice. And hopefully you'll get the hang of things.

What Not To Talk About

What not to talk about. OK, so by now, you know, approaching talking and the two important aspects of making a good first conversation, namely confidence in emotional questions and answers, that should work very nicely for you and you should probably have it handled. However, it is good practice that you use caution as sometimes you can accidentally say something that would take all your efforts downhill based on a single simple mistake. So instead of regretting it, it's better to go over some tips before saying anything at all.

This chapter will just straight up mention and explain the things you should avoid talking about since it's not really rocket science. Always remember that the first impressions are important, make the most of it count, the first and foremost thing is that you should avoid being negative, duh, avoid things like how your life is falling apart, how you hate your life, your lack of friends and so on. These things will destroy your already president. Confident, likable guy. Image shifting from a positive to a sudden negative vibe is a huge red flag for girls, and they'd want to avoid you faster than, well, anything, really. Moreover, remember, nobody likes being around a negative person. Avoid this one at all costs.

Do not talk about money questions like how much do you make are some very personal questions and asking them on a first encounter does not make any sense. Apart from that, it's a very rude thing to ask. And people in general are usually uncomfortable talking about it, even with friends, let alone a girl meeting a stranger for the first time. The gentleman's rule of first encounters is to not bring up politics when meeting anyone for the first time, and rightly so, there are some conversations that might be strong enough to break everything you've already so far established. It might also lead to an awkward silence or even a small political outburst from her. Yeah, you'd want to avoid that on a first meeting.

Similarly, religion has its place with politics, asking straight up personal questions like their belief in God or in other religions are considered straight up uncomfortable for a whole lot of people. You'd want your first encounter to go with minimum conflict whatsoever. Bringing this up might just ruin it for you. The next one might come as sort of a surprise, but avoid bringing up her physical appearance even if it is a compliment. Though this rule can be bent on some occasions, it's a good idea to avoid it for two reasons. The first being that if she's a really pretty girl, she's probably heard that she's beautiful a million times by other guys already and is probably sick and tired of it and might be looking for something new or different. This acts as a shortcut of sorts and actually keeps her interested in you because you haven't fallen on your knees for her already. And it actually sparked some interest from her.

At least that's the case most of the time. Second, it's weird to get such compliments from total strangers on a first encounter. You can, however, give subtle signs like comments about it to keep it friendly without overdoing it. This is one place a lot of guys unknowingly fail really badly. And the last thing that's purely about you, don't be self-centered and talk about yourself or your likes constantly give her room to express herself as well because of two reasons. The first being that it keeps her interested and the second that you're trying to have a conversation and not a declaration. Keep that in mind at all times and you should be good to go.

As a conclusion, remember that you can bring up pretty much anything, but there are certain things to avoid. These are topics that in very rare cases can be brought up. But from experience, it's better not to. As always, I hope you find this chapter insightful and hopefully it will be of some use to you guys. Good luck and see you next time.

chapter on how to keep her interested, you're engaged in a conversation, and at this point you're OK with anything except blowing this up. The fact is that you've made it this far and you've already half established yourself as a likable, positive guy. She'll definitely start to like you just a little bit. The final and most crucial part of completing a successful conversation is the conversation itself. Introduce yourself, give her your name and one line that defines you at your best or in a funny way, for example, referring back to the coffee shop example, you can say something like this. Hi, I'm Johnny, avid coffee lover, slash engineer, etc.. Do be honest about it, though.

The last thing you'd want is for her to be a coffee lover or two. And you're being forced to agree to spend every Tuesday morning over coffee or you'll eventually give in and admit you lied just to get with her, damaging what you have in the process. Just don't overdo it and you should be good. Getting to know her in your brief introduction will prompt her to engage in an equally brief or funny introduction. If she does that, that's a really great sign and points out that she might be interested in having a conversation with you.

After all, the next step is to talk and get to the real part of the conversation, going talk about something, anything. If you're indecisive, use your observation to find something the both of you might have in common. Is she carrying a magazine both of you are interested in or referring back to the coffee shop example, the flavor she's having, what she has paired with it? It's essential that whatever you bring up, make sure that you have sufficient knowledge and interest in it yourself. You wouldn't want a boring conversation about her shoes after you compliment them and you wouldn't want her in the same situation. Like if you bring up Star Wars, the basic principle is to keep a two way conversation going. Talk to her about anything around you. If you feel like the both of you might be into something only to find out she isn't, it would be a good idea to shift the conversation.

Similarly, you can bring up stuff like current events or ongoing stuff. It doesn't necessarily have to be politics. It could be as simple as the new Game of Thrones episode or something. You could talk about food in general, anything, really. Remember, it's not what you say, but how you say it. And yes, somewhere down the line, you'll also be able to bring up Star Wars, too. If things go well, just give that time. A way to keep the conversation going and keep her interested is to adopt the Ford method, it's a widely available and an acceptable reputed and proven method that actually works to break it down. Ford is an abbreviation for family, occupation, recreation and dreams. It can be used as a powerful tool to keep conversation going. And interesting. And if at any time you feel like you're running out of things to talk about, you can always come back to the Ford method.

The first thing you can talk about is his family instead of directly just asking about it and seeming very creepy. In doing so, you can refer to it and bring it up in multiple different ways. You can look around the room and make an observation like how the girl next to you reminds you of your sister because she talks too much and you just find it funny because you haven't seen her in a while. Or the old guy who reminds you of your dad because he's always trying to fit in and you miss him like in the previous chapters, share a small story that brings out emotion and prompts her with a question like, do you have an older, talkative sister?

This is a subtle and very clever way of shifting the conversation to family. You can also make a straight up assumption like you've been an only child, am I right? Stuff like this is a step towards the both of you opening up and talking on a relatable level, both which are huge steps in the right direction. Occupation should be the next thing on the priority list. Ask her what she does for a living organ. Ask him before she answers. Assume what she does if she gives you an answer like she's an accountant or a student, instead of making some generic and bland questions like, oh, where do you work or study or how much do you make? What's your GPA? Those are informative questions, something we'd want to avoid because it leads to a dead end, which you might want to ask. Are questions like do you enjoy it or relate on an emotional level? Like I've always been inspired by that.

This encourages other emotional responses, something you're better able to connect with and a greater chance of finding a more common interest. You feel like that's not enough. You can talk about recreation, even a generic question like what do you like to do in your spare time? Can work like a charm in other ways and engage in questions like do you like books or what is your favorite TV series and why these things can trigger her into taking the lead of the conversation. Even if you don't know anything about her favorite pastime, say, fishing, you can ask her what she feels about it or like how she enjoys it. This can get her to open up about herself.

Somewhat of a great sign that things are going great. The final and most emotionally deepest thing to talk about is dreams. For this can bring up some of the most heart to heart conversations. This is one thing you should only bring up when you've known each other for a while, or when you find you'll be spending time together long and alone. Ask questions like How does she give her life meaning? Or What does she hope to achieve before finally dying? Tell her about your passions as well. You can also pair this with the recreation part of the Ford method for a combined result. These lines may come across as cheesy, but in the right setting, like a quiet atmosphere, it can be one of the best conversations you two might ever have. So use this one wisely because it is the last of the Ford methods.

As homework, practice the Ford method with friends and family members, see what interesting conversations you can strike up and try molding it to your liking, go out and apply it towards new people as well, make some friends along the way and have fun. The next important thing to do will be to get her number and text her and we'll get into that in the next chapters. Until then, we'll see you guys later.

Getting Her Number

chapter 11, getting her number. So now you had a conversation and you really seem to like this girl and get the feeling that she also likes you back as a person. But for some reason or another, it seems like the whole thing will be coming to an end and you two might be parting ways really soon. Getting her number is the best way to make sure you two can stay in touch or ever meet up again. It's one of the simplest and easiest things to do in this Book. Yet so many people can go wrong here. And that's where I'm going to step in to save the day when in the middle of a conversation, basically the peak of where you both are equally involved and are having fun, you could say something like, oh, man, you're really fun to be around.

We should definitely meet up sometime soon if you're OK with it. Of course, while pulling out your cell phone, make sure this doesn't happen at the start. But instead, somewhere along the middle to end part of your interaction at the peak of conversations, girls feel more confident in giving you their number and they really start to like you make the most of it. The only downside, more like the prerequisite to this method, is that you need to be good at reading your surroundings and detecting her body language. Another method could be that you ask around if you suddenly realize you have to go say something like, Oh wow, time really flies when talking about some really cool stuff with some really cool people. I'd love to continue the conversation some time. If you're up for it, we should meet up some time. Is that cool?

If she feels the same way, then you may proceed in asking her for her number. This one is effective, subtle and natural and is very easy to bring about. Just don't be nervous when doing so. Remember, you're the confident, likable guy. Act like it. The third way, yet the least recommended of the three is to invite her to something cool you have or you know about. For example, if you guys happen to be discussing food and pizza in particular, and you happen to know this amazing and underrated pizza joint, you can always invite her for dinner with you. You can say something along the lines of speaking of pizza, have you tried this pizza place? They make the most amazing pizzas in town and a lot of people don't know about it. If she seems interested, arrange a meeting there with something like tell you what, let's meet up there sometime and I'll show you around the place. I'm getting the feeling you'll love it.

This is present, open and welcoming. You can have any similar well crafted lines like these. It is, however, important to stay true to yourself and say what you like. Don't end up inviting her to the fanciest place in town. Anywhere where the both of you could have an enjoyable time will do so perfectly. And those are the methods to get you working. It is, however, recommended to go over some precautions as well. The first, like mentioned, get her number at an appropriate time. Asking for it in the first few minutes is just creepy. Another thing to avoid is that you shouldn't ask her for it. When the conversation is coming to awkward pauses, those moments tend to give her the impression you two have absolutely nothing in common.

She'll feel really uneasy if you make it more uncomfortable for her by pressuring her to give you her number under any circumstances. Do not trick her into giving your number. It's a very rude thing to do and well, it practically speaks for itself. Similarly, do not pressure her for it. If she is unwilling to, she's made up her mind. There's next to nothing you can do about it. And finally, when you do get her number, don't be overly excited about it or let it show by exclaiming yes or similar things. That gives the whole impression as if that were your only objective. Instead, play it cool with saying something like Awesome thanks or positive smile. And that's pretty much all there is to getting a girl's number. Naturally, you should go out and try it on people, but do not leave them hanging. Once you get there, no promising to meet up or something, go along with it. You might just end up making friends with people. Go ahead and do this, and I'll see you next time.

Reaching Out On Social Media: Snapchat

chapter 12, reaching out on social media Snapchat, this chapter looks towards two situations, one in which you've just met a girl and the other in which both of you haven't. Both of them followed the same tips and are applicable to both situations before we get started. It's worth pointing out that for both cases, you don't want to follow her on multiple social media platforms all at once. That will only give off the impression that you have nothing better to do in life or that you're straight up obsessed with her. Yeah, not the vibe we worked so hard to achieve. Right. Once you are at her, avoid snapping her things immediately and don't send text like hi or what's up? Because there's a good chance that she might just leave, it is red.

Remember, on platforms like Snapchat, people don't respond to every snap. So she doesn't don't worry about it. Send her snaps that you would normally send to your other friends. Don't make it like she's the only one who's going to get them and just keep it casual. Don't do it too frequently, but just enough for her to get to know you a bit. And she might even start snapping back this way. You'll make it into a recent list and that's a good sign. She's a really hot girl. Chances are she gets a lot of snaps from a lot of other guys trying to impress her, which she'll probably be sick of already.

Sending her normal regular snaps is a far better way to get things going for you that will also make you stand out from the bunch. Be sure not to overuse it, though, as she might get annoyed. So keep it to about a maximum of about two snaps for 24 hours and you should be good. A great sign is that she starts responding to them. Even if the snaps aren't specific to her, it's more likely to engage the both of you in a conversation. The next step is for you to respond or react to some of her stories. Remember, keeping things casual is the key here. You can respond to some casual topic in her snap, something like if she posts a chapter of her having coffee, saying something like, wow, that's one of the fanciest looking coffee pictures I've seen in a while, that's good enough for her to give out a response. And you'll be heading towards a potential conversation with her.

Keep comments about her out of it, though. Like suppose you post a picture with her friend and you end up commenting something like, both of you look gorgeous. You'd most likely want to avoid that along the same lines. One very important thing to do is to not ask for nudes ever. Just don't girls hate it and it just makes you look like. And let's be honest, nobody finds that attractive. So please just avoid that one at all times. One amazing way to get the both of you closer is that you eventually work your way to a Snapchat streak. That way you can send snaps to each other every day. You'll have an excuse to do so. Just don't overdo it.

With more than two snaps a day, people just get tired of looking at the same boring routine you might have. So try to make that last longer by limiting your snaps. Those are the most straightforward tips you should know about the basic dos and don'ts of approaching a girl. As always, you can try your way according to what the situation looks like, but so far I'm sure all of you out there have a basic idea on how and what to do. I'll see you guys in the next chapter.

Reaching Out On Social Media: Instagram

chapter 13, reaching out on social media Instagram, the previous chapter focused on adding a girl on Snapchat, this one as a continuation, will take it a step further with adding her on another social media platform, which is Instagram. The basic fundamentals so far have been the same, but this chapter goes into some specific details that you may want to look into before going in to approach a girl you're not friends with. But you do know her from work, school or the neighborhood.

The best thing to do is like a couple of her pictures, not one, because you'll probably not even notice it, not more than two, because it'll make you seem either desperate or creepy, too, because it's normal. And she's more likely to single you out and remember your name. She might even go to your profile. And like one of your pictures after that's happened, you can DM her something funny related to her picture, but not something about her.

Looks like, wow, look high because that's going to make you look like a creep. And we've already been over that several times. Going to something like this place looks breathtaking. Where is it that's likely to get her to respond to you? And there you have it. The conversation started. This might not work on one of those models who have thousands of followers, though, and it's most likely hit or miss, so don't stress out about it too much. It's also a good idea to actually have good pictures on your page. You can go ahead and filter and edit them to the max, but be sure not to overdo them to make it easier. Get one of your female friends to help you out with that, have pictures that actually make you look good in the pictures that do not include you. Be sure that they stand out and are well captured. There are plenty of tutorials out there that can help you with those apps, too.

I prefer snap speed as it's simple and extremely easy to use. Also, it's free. So there's that when you do go on to like her pictures, making sure you only like the recent ones for older ones would make her feel like you're stalking her. And that will make her feel uncomfortable. Based on some research, people are more likely to react. Remember your name, if you like their selfies instead of their other kinds of photos, take full advantage of that and combine it with the tips already mentioned before liking her recent pictures. That'll be sure to make her remember your name. If you feel like going soft with just a couple of likes and hoping that she'll respond might be a long shot, you could always leave a comment.

Instead, it's very likely she'll respond to that. Make sure your comment is well timed, clever, witty or funny. Anything that does not make you look creepy or like a desperate person. We've already been over this that you can talk or comment anything. Remember when I told you it's not about what you say, but how you say it? Well, it applies the same here to what I mentioned before, the well timed and innovative comment, nothing fancy and you'll be fine if things go well further. You can always dream of making the use of your Instagram stories and use that to like Snapchat. Be sure not to use it too much with selfies because people often have a tendency to get sick of it really quickly. Make sure to embrace the days that you do look good and post accordingly.

If things don't work out by any of the above methods, it's healthy to just take the hint that she doesn't want to proceed any further than what's already happened. And it's best that you leave it at that. Don't waste time in pursuing someone who wouldn't do the same back. Remember, you have a reputation and you should hold it up with pride. It's natural to get shot down like that, but if it's not meant to be, it should be dropped altogether. Knowing that you did all that you could have possibly done. I hope you guys found this useful. And I'll see you in the next chapter.

Texting

chapter 14 texting, most guys are actually really confused when texting a girl, they would often text something, have a conversation going for a while until she stopped replying and then would just stand there and contemplate what they did wrong or trying to find out why she isn't replying anymore. This happens to most guys more than you think, and there are many reasons for that. The first is that she may not want to carry on further because the conversation has reached its natural end and they see no reason to keep talking to you. So it's pretty common for that to happen.

The best way to get over this is that you have other important things in your life. Like I've mentioned in the previous chapters, it's a good idea to have other life objectives than just trying to pursue a girl that would make you look less clingy and your texting conversations can be better. You should also text back at your own pace and not always instantly. Do not text her very frequently, as in all day, every day. Limit your texting to only when you think it's a good idea. Nobody likes an overly clingy person and it's just annoying. And if she has any good impression of you, it will likely be overshadowed by this happening and it'll all go to waste.

Like I mentioned earlier, you should have better things to do with your life instead of obsessing over her all the time. Another thing to avoid is to be dependent or act like you're crying over text about her, not replying to you fast enough or canceling any certain plans you might have had. It's a good idea to let it go and ignore the whole thing instead of going on a full rant. Remember standards. Next up, we'll look at how to text, you can send her anything random could be a small, interesting question, something funny or any kind of question about her that'll get you a reply and start a conversation, keep it a simple one and have a normal sized one, basically, until it comes to a natural end.

When that happens, just stop replying instead of clinging onto it. That'll make you look less desperate and would make her feel more comfortable talking to you. Do this from time to time and you're likely able to develop an understanding. Ask her about her day or the tiny things in her life later on, and that'll help you to go further. After you and texting for a while, it's fairly obvious that guys like to overcomplicate things like how long she's taking to reply, how many emojis she's using, but it's not that hard and quite simple. I Want you to have good texting momentum. It's good to ask her out after about a week or so, which basically was our purpose, make plans, invite her to this new place we discovered or anything you feel might get her interested either in meeting you or spending time with you instead of waiting around for the perfect moment. It's good to just go for it. If she comes up with an excuse, it's OK to ignore it.

The first time it could be legitimate. You could try asking her out again, preferably after a week or so if she gives an excuse, but is OK with rescheduling plans. That means you should keep going. But if she turns you down again, just ignore and move on with the fact in mind that you should end things right there and focus on your life instead. Now for a few tips on actually texting her, the most important thing is to not lose your charm, keep her interested and make her smile over text. You can do that by lightly teasing her, making fun of yourself sometimes, or try guessing her answers with funny logic. It could be any one of those things done right. And you can leave quite an impression.

One simple rule is to not over do anything, have the right blend of text that will have humor, response and wit. And that's basically it. Texting isn't hard, but guys make it hard for themselves. So remember, there aren't many do's in texting, but just a handful of don'ts to live by and everything should work out just fine. We'll see you guys in the next chapter.

Misc: Flirting via Text

chapter 15, flirting via text. Some people find this as a way to keep the person you're texting with engaged. Others find it to ease the tension. Flirting during a text conversation can be used as a powerful tool to do just that and much more. This chapter focuses on just that. First off, remember, it's not essential. You waste half your day going through the Internet looking for that perfect text message. You'll find no such thing. While some might come off as appealing, they might not work for you.

The best resource comes from within you because only you know how the situation fares. It might be a good idea to often skim through some from time to time, but only to serve as an inspiration for you to get creative with the situation that might arise. But remember, it should primarily be from you, preferably a blend of humor and sarcasm with the occasional tease. The first step is to be original. I know it's hard, but once you actually pull something off, you won't be the only one impressed. The girl reading it might be pleasantly delighted by your creativity. Remember, the goal is to make her smile and leave a subtle hint of your liking towards her. You know her better than some lines on the Internet. Just be original and try to make some interesting observations about her to incorporate these three things and you might have a good line working your way.

Another thing you can do is just ask an open question, try to keep it open ended and give her room to express herself, just try not to keep it too open ended or too personal. Too sudden. It's a good idea to watch out for your spelling and grammar. Good grammar really leaves an impact. Realize it's often the little things that count. Don't worry too much about it, though. Anything that sounds normal enough is good to go, but avoid some obvious mistakes. There are plenty of free online resources available. If you feel like you lack in this area. A simple Google search can do that just fine for you. Understand that subtlety is the key in these situations.

You might not want to come across as too strong when texting her, giving her the impression that you really want to be with her. But instead you should remember that flirting over text is not so different from flirting in real life. You should still relax and take it easy. If you want to be successful, flirt to keep your attention, you may tease her over little things. Teasing is a great way to get fast responses. It could be anything like her watching a silly movie to her weird habits. Make sure she knows you're joking. Of course, emojis in this case can help you express yourself better and keep it light.

The last thing you would want to do is harder. Something like I can't believe you were into those Barbie movies. That's so hilariously cute is a perfect example. A useful way is to use her name often; it can really help get things going and bring out a certain spark of sorts. Use this to show you care for her in situations like if she's sick or not feeling well, a text like asking if she's better using her name is sure to put a smile on her face and make her feel a bit better. Do compliment her occasionally too. The basic purpose of messaging is going to be making plans or keeping a like connection during a separation period.

Do not let it be a substitute for an actual relationship itself. Both learning via text may be fun for the both of you. It's no proper substitute for the long term. Do meet up if you want things to go further, otherwise you're pretty much living on borrowed time. The basic key here is to be yourself. As generic as it sounds, it's actually the most noteworthy advice I can give. The girl will like you for who you are. Don't come across as someone you're not, otherwise you might just start doubting the both of you show you care t's. And don't be rude. Those are the dos and don'ts of this chapter. I really hope you do good in these things and I'm sure you guys have it handled. And as always, I'll see you in the next chapter.

Carrying On

chapter 16 carrying on this chapter marks the last of this Book and will primarily focus on the last thing to a lasting relationship with a girl, which is often difficult for some people, while others can manage it relatively with ease. It's maintaining an active relationship with the girl you've met and have a liking for. The important thing to do is to make sure that you do have a part in her life that can be done with involvement. You don't necessarily have to hang out with her 24/7 or too little that you become non-existent, but just enough that the both of you are involved enough to know what goes on in each other's lives. That clearly may be subject to the situation.

You guys could always sit together in class or often carpool together to work or maybe even have lunch together on a daily basis. But these are the things that you need to realize for yourself. If she had the same liking towards you, there's no reason that what I've said cannot or should not happen. If it's not as close, you can still stay involved with the little things like saying hi or asking for a small favor once in a while, check up on her if she's sick and that kind of stuff, she'll have you as a person who's close to her. The next thing is to ask her out again. The frequency may be dependent on your situation of how exactly your relationship stands with her. It could be from every weekend to once a month or maybe even longer. If you do want that active involvement, make sure it's never more than one month. It doesn't necessarily just have to be the two of you either. Mutual friends can work too.

The point is that the both of you should have fun together, try to be a part of each other's hobbies, too. If she's into watching old movies, ask for suggestions and maybe even have a movie night arranged for one both of you haven't seen. If you're into gaming, have a game night with a friend. Try things out together. The point here is to experience things together, share those experiences and make a connection with them over these experiences. That's sure to bring even the most distant of cases together. Be a good listener. If you are upset, talk about it. Take her out to coffee or maybe a park where the both of you can have a private conversation and listen to what she has to say.

Be supportive of what she says. Make her feel she can count on you and be that person she'll look up to in her time of need. This situation can also apply in a reverse role scenario. It's bound to make her approach you when she sees you upset. Talk to her about it. She'll always try your best to keep your spirits high or find a fix for whatever you're going through. Just maintain communication. Thank you. When you overcome it. And sure you're happy about her in your life. Text often when over a long distance, a funny picture or a reminder of what you saw or anything, make sure you guys have something to talk about. Having a small inside joke can help asking her about her day or what she's up to.

Anything really just knows it's all the cost of staying involved and that's what we want to do. This officially marks the end of the Book. I really hope this was worth it to you guys. Remember, it's not rocket science, but just a game of a handful of qualities and thinking skills that can be adopted by enough practice, never settle for less and always have a respectable standard. Never force a girl to do anything and be you while doing so. I'm sure that you guys have this handled. Don't forget to give this a five star rating and reach out to me. If you think the Book is lacking anywhere, that's it. And I'll see you all in the next Book.

Small Business Lead Generation Using Proven Cold Email Tactics

Hi, Welcome to Lead Generation and the effective appointment making online workshop. Learn innovative and outstanding skills to help you Prospekt effectively become a professional sales prospector, perhaps one of the most important roles of marketing and sales as creating sales opportunities. This prospecting workshop focuses on finding more prospects by teaching you how to discover who your real ideal prospect is and where to find them.

Learn how to create empathy and step into your prospects shoes, whether you're a B2B or B2C. In this Book, you will discover with social media the people you need and want what you're offering. You will discover how to maximize LinkedIn, Facebook, Twitter, YouTube and Pinterest to find prospects who are ready and willing to buy from you. You will successfully master the right way to make an approach on social media platforms. Learn to build rapport and positive interaction.

Many salespeople drive potential prospects on social media away by making inappropriate approaches. I'm sure you've sort of saved some already discovered a unique approach which will uncover the risks of falling foul of GDP. With cold emails, you will learn how, with permission based marketing, to get in front of more prospects. Imagine knowing how to warm up your cold prospects out there waiting for your call. Learn the magic of how to conduct virtual appointments online, which will get results. This workshop is based on practical skills that get results that will fill your pipeline with qualified prospects.

Cold calling and appointment making is usually the least like part of any sales. Job prospects do not like receiving unwanted phone calls, resulting in rejection and frustration for the salesperson. When you take on board the lessons in this workshop, you'll be amused before you're halfway through. Learn how you can build rapport and create empathy quickly on the telephone. With the emphasis on results, this hands-on workshop will ensure success and appointment making. Listen to me make a phone call at this workshop. Hear me get past the gatekeeper smoothly and easily. Kolkhoz usually fails because your prospects don't hear any value in your content.

You will learn how to have a worthwhile conversation that will bring value to your prospect. Join us today and watch your pipeline fill and grow with qualified prospects enabling you to close more sales, exceed your sales target and increase your earning potential. This workshop is about your success.

Why Prospect

What is prospecting and why do we have salespeople need to prospect prospecting is the process of initiating and developing new business by searching for potential buyers, customers, our clients, for our products, our services. The idea is to move these prospects to the sales process until you win their business. The term prospector refers to the efforts of individuals trying to find gold by Scandi Creek riverbeds and rocks. These people were prospecting for valuable nuggets of gold.

Often they were misled by fool's gold, which we can be as well when we are prospecting for prospective clients. That is what we do in sales as modern day sales, prospectors sifting through large lists of potential prospects to try and uncover those who have the need for our services, the authority to buy, they have the budget and they're ready to buy the engagement. Sally is about getting someone to buy our products or services, but we cannot advance our sales unless we can separate the fool's gold from those nuggets of valuable gold.

We need to start by focusing on how to find and develop and qualify our potential customers. This is prospecting. Prospecting is the number one challenge or issue you face when it comes to growing sales. Without prospects, you have no prospects. Let me repeat that. Without prospects, you have no prospects. Prospecting is an important part of the sales process as it helps to develop a pipeline of potential customers in prospecting. We have suspects and prospects. Allow me to explain. We start with suspects, suspects are individuals or companies you believe may want what you offer, you suspect there might be customers, but you're unsure. So what you need to do is to increase their awareness and familiarity with your business. Once they are aware, we need to determine if they might or will buy in the future. On the other hand, prospects.

Our suspect you have contacted and you've established that they might be interested in buying from you at some point, we will discuss and demonstrate in this workshop how to qualify suspects and discover if they are indeed prospects. We will learn how to discover if they have the need for our product, our services. Do they have the economic wherewithal to invest in our products or services? Is the prospect someone in authority who can make the decision to buy? And is the timing right for them? In this Book, you will learn to uncover and discover who is in the market for products and services. By learning to ask the right questions in this Book, you will discover prospecting techniques which will remove the need for cold calling by warming up your prospects and then engaging in a way where they'll be waiting to hear from you. Prospecting techniques you may not have tried. These techniques will get you results when you learn how to use them properly and the next lesson you will learn how to set some prospecting goals on this Book will help you achieve them.

Mindset

A model of success, what characteristics does a successful sales person have? He's got the right attitude, he's got the right skills, he's got the right knowledge,forms, habits. Your emotions are created by three forces. Force One is a personal physiology of biochemistry, structure and movement. Force two is a pattern of focus and belief. Which values, rules and identity for three is a pattern of language. In questions, metaphors and incantations, our success or failure is determined by a set of sequences. Our behavior determines our feelings, feelings produce attitudes that are responsible for our beliefs, and that is how we are programming ourselves.

The question is, are you moving toward success or away from failure? Three facts. Fact one, the only person in your life who determines your success is you to fight all successful people, take charge of their thinking fact for no one gets successful alone. Belief systems, empowering beliefs or limiting beliefs. Are you motivated to say what you want or to move away from what you don't want? If we don't know where we are going, any road will take us acknowledging our emotions, we need to assert ourselves. Hi, where are our behaviors?

Are we able to empathize with people? Can we solve the problem? Perth are equals, which means event, perfect response equals the outcome. How do you respond to the events in your life? Assertiveness. When the going gets tough, can you assert yourself when necessary and speak up? Can you negotiate effectively? Can you co-exist with diverse personality styles? Can you handle constructive criticism? Persistence, persistence is the difference between knowing and doing nothing in this world can take the place of persistence talent. Well, now nothing is more common than unsuccessful people with talent. Genius will not.

Unrewarding genius is almost a proverb. Education will not. The world is full of educated, derelict persistence and determination alone are an impotent Calvin Coolidge, 30th president of the United States. What are your intentions to achieve your goals? What do you intend to do when? Functional fantasy's, anything worth doing? Is worth doing. I am responsible for my own results. I cannot blame anyone else for my results. Work is play, make your work from. And every adversity hides the seeds of victory. Things don't get better by accident, they get better by appropriate action. Commitment. It is the key to excellence. An old Ziggler said, If I give others what they want and need, they will give me what I want. I need. Now is the definition of selling, making a decision, taking action. What is your decision? What actions will you take?

Do you sincerely want to grow your steel to make a quantum leap, to grow your sales? Stephen Covey encouraged us to begin with the end in mind. What do you want to achieve? Set yourself a 90 day objective based on the following criteria, set practical objectives. Are they realistic, attainable, known and understood? Are you clear about what you want to achieve, set your objectives and have X value of high value prospects and your goals? And then the next 90 days, how many low value prospects will you be working on? Be clear about what you want. What do you want to achieve? Turn your want into a goal. Right, your gold don't catch three to five gold cards, right, put your gold out on the card, what you want to achieve, keep the card in your wallet or purse and read the card at least three times a day. Abraham Maslow said, if you plan to be anything less than you are capable of being, you will probably be unhappy all the days of your life.

Seven Habits of Highly Effective Salespeople

A vote that applies to all sales people is the seven habits of successful people by the list. Stephen covid. Let's look at the seven habits that apply to you in the CEO's world. How about number one, be proactive. Take action, nothing happens till we take action. We are steps people can use many excuses not to take action. Being proactive ensures that we take responsibility for our actions. We have the ability to respond appropriately, intention plus attention times. Our belief equals results. Put simply, what we are focusing on every day.

Focus on what you can do today, not what you can do. Number two begins with the end in mind and an old sales trainer told me many years ago, if you don't know where you're going, any road will take you. Whether you have a job, or whether you're prospecting, having the sales, maybe making a presentation of your objectives, what do you want to achieve? What are your intentions for this activity? What is your end goal? Number three, it is put first things first, put first things first, you've probably heard of the easy 21 20 percent of your action produces 80 percent of the results of knowing which of those actions you need to take focus on what is important to you to get you where you want to be and let go of the all important. This quadrant teaches you time management, less than a minute to discover where in the quadrant you need to focus, starting with what is urgent and what is important, working on what matters most then come to have a number for habit number four tells us to think when when we will be more successful, when we help our clients succeed, we both need to win.

If the client loses, we lose. And for habit number five, number five, seek first to understand, then to be understood. The essence of qualifying the client is inquiry, asking the right questions to better understand customers. What they really want is helping clients close the gap from where they are now to where they want to be. Having sex is synergise, we need to be creative, flexible and adaptable in matching what we do with the client, wants and needs to give clients insights to solve our problems. And finally, the story of the Witcover. The need to sharpen the saw, and this is No.7, the story of the woodcutter who needed to chop down 20 trees a day, but if was too busy to take the time to sharpen his ax and we all know what would happen if he didn't stop to sharpen his ax will help you sharpen your ax by learning and growing your sales.

Prospecting Goals and Strategy

Hi, In this chapter on prospecting, we will focus on Saffy prospecting gold and setting the strategy for success to achieve success and prospecting. We need to know what it is we want to achieve and how we are going to get there. That is our sales in relation to our sales goal. Two simple questions. How much bigram do we need to set realistic prospecting activity gold? Stephen Covey coined the phrase Begin with the end in mind. You need to set realistic prospecting activity gold.

Let's walk through the mouths. Wolf, the best effective method for stopping prospecting gold maybe is to start with the financial gold. But you want to achieve or you may want to determine how many prospects you need in your pipeline. Remember that prospects, our companies, our people, we have qualified as having the need for our product or service. They have the authority to buy. It's in their budget and they're in the market right now. I suggest that you set the 30, 60, 90 day goals to take us from where we are now to where we want to be, beginning with the end of my 90 day objectives: practical, realistic, attainable, measurable, known and understood. So setting your goals for your number of prospects in 90 days, qualified prospects in the pipeline. Can you have X prospects in 90 days? So that is your goal. One of the most effective methods for setting your prospecting goals is to start with financial goals that you want to achieve. Let's use this example, let's say you have a goal of earning. Sixty K in this business year to 60 K in this business year, you need to sell six hundred K worth of business. So let's say your average day is three K. That means you need to take 22 sales, your next calculation is a number of prospects you will need to speak to to get 60 Minutes.

Let's assume that your ratio of conversion with prospects to qualified meetings is five to one. That means you need to have 300 conversions to get 60, 80, 90 days with only 65 working days. You need to be contacting five to six prospects a day. You'll find that she's attached to work and you're prospecting with. So work on your personal prospecting with the sheet provided, how do you organize yourself to do this? When prospecting, you'll need consistency and focus. And in this Book we'll show you exactly how to do this. But consistency, focus. And Brazilian's, the methods I teach you will keep you focused.

Keep your consistency, I'm going to keep your Rassilon. It's about how you structure your day, your day may look like this. Start today with your inbox, then go to your leads and prospects, read through LinkedIn, develop your contacts called prospects, make appointments to the voicemail, engage new prospects and follow up emails, nurture leads, email, phone and face to face meetings. We will show you exactly how to do all this. This is your strategy. Having established your goal for the next 90 days, you need a plan of action, a strategy to get you from where you are to where you want to be.

Handling Rejection

The fear of rejection is one of those things we need to learn to overcome salespeople. How can we deal with rejection when we're a prospect? Most salespeople who tell you do not take it personally. This is always possible after our emotions get in the way, some of it too simple not to take it personally. You get distressed over rejection. Big part of the reason is that we do take it personally. The imposter syndrome, Clexane, and we start beating ourselves up. We feel as if we are being rejected on a deep personal level, as if the prospect is really rejecting us as a human being. Part of the problem is that we take ourselves too seriously.

Let's think about rejection. Really. Is it just someone to say no to your offer? Think about the last cold call you received and rejected that big of a deal. Right. You told the person your reason for not buying. I moved on with your life. You probably don't even remember the sales person's name. This is exactly how it is with your prospects. If they reject you, they won't even remember who you are or work for. And it's not that serious. When we were teenagers, we got rejected by that. You buy our guard in the class. When we look back now, we can laugh at ourselves we can't control. But prospects say or do. We can only control our own actions, our own activities.

We can only control what we say and do and how frequently we do. How can we control what we say? That's why we get rejected. We get checked out for many reasons and we look at some of them. First of all, they may only suspect they're not qualified prospects. We haven't established a need or perhaps they're not in the market right now. A major reason we get rejection is we do not have a worthwhile conversation that demonstrates value. One of the major benefits of this Book is to teach you how to have a worthwhile conversation which adds value to your prospects. I will show you in this Book how to offer insight on your column.

Anyone who has succeeded in life has overcome rejections. Thomas Edison, who felt many times when inventing the electric light bulb, didn't give up. He went on to win and found that carbon filament that would light the light bulb, Walt Disney, he got fired from the Kansas City Star because he apparently lacked imagination. Oprah Winfrey, who has become very successful, got fired from a news supporting job because she couldn't separate her emotions from her news stories. Michael Jordan, one of the greatest basketball players, got dropped from his high school basketball team. But then they give up.

No, they kept going and they were resilient. So that's mic rejection, the key. This will become a game changer for you. Reaction is going to happen no matter what you do. So just let's make it again. Say that one sales person has a goal of setting five appointments. Today, an enormous sales person has a goal of getting 50 rejections. The first salesperson struggles to get five appointments. He ends up spending time away from a staff desk, drinking coffee, feeling rejected, and the second salesperson focuses on getting 50 rejections. He doesn't give up when he hears no, just says next and is motivated to move on.

Trust me when I tell you that the quickest way to set yourself apart from everyone else is to actively seek out rejection, seek out news after hearing. Yes is the easy part. Anybody can do that hearing. No, it's empowering. You can play this game another way, set yourself a goal of getting 10 no's in a row. If someone says yes to you and says your fifth or sixth call, you have to start again to get your 10 no's in Earl. Let me finish this chapter with the story about one of the greatest salespeople ever, a Labor frontbencher who wrote some of the most empowering CEOs books in the 30s. If Carnegie encouraged Frank Thatcher to write his first bestselling book, How I Raised Myself From Failure to Success in Selling.

He went on to write, How I multiply my income and happiness in selling. Frank became successful as he counted, known as successes, he knew with each, though he was getting closer to his goal. We will all experience rejection is how we decide to process it and when at the prospect. We treat it like Frank Thatcher and see that your next no is one step towards success.

Summary

That's summarized in our last four chapters. Prospecting is the process of initiating and developing new business by searching for potential buyers, customers clamoring for your products or services. That is to move these prospects through the sales process until you win their business. The term prospector refers to the efforts of individuals trying to find gold in the old Klondike. We start off with suspect suspects. Are individuals or companies you believe may want what you offer?

Prospect, on the other hand, are suspects you have contacted and have established that they might be interested in buying from you at some point they have a need. We will discuss and demonstrate in this workshop how to qualify suspects and discover if they are indeed prospects to achieve success and prospecting. We need to know what it is we want to achieve and how we are going to get there. Let us ask ourselves in relation to our sales goal, two simple questions. How much, Byran?

Overcoming the fear of rejection is one of those things we need to overcome as salespeople. How can we deal with rejection and why do we get rejection? We get rejected because we do not have a worthwhile conversation that shows value rejection is going to happen no matter what you do. So let's make it a game. Set yourself a goal of getting 10 of those in a row if someone says yes. At number six, you have to start again to get 10 no's. You'll become more motivated knowing that you're winning the game of prospecting and achieving your goals. See you in the next segment when we discover who your customer is. That's summarized in our last four chapters. Prospecting is the process of initiating and developing new business by searching for potential buyers, customers clamoring for your products or services. That is to move these prospects through the sales process until you win their business. The term prospector refers to the efforts of individuals trying to find gold in the old Klondike. We start off with suspect suspects. Are individuals or companies you believe may want what you offer?

Prospect, on the other hand, are suspects you have contacted and have established that they might be interested in buying from you at some point they have a need. We will discuss and demonstrate in this workshop how to qualify suspects and discover if they are indeed prospects to achieve success and prospecting. We need to know what it is we want to achieve and how we are going to get there. Let us ask ourselves in relation to our sales goal, two simple questions. How much, Byran? Overcoming the fear of rejection is one of those things we need to overcome as salespeople. How can we deal with rejection and why do we get rejection?

We get rejected because we do not have a worthwhile conversation that shows value rejection is going to happen no matter what you do. So let's make it a game. Set yourself a goal of getting 10 of those in a row if someone says yes. At number six, you have to start again to get 10 no's. You'll become more motivated knowing that you're winning the game of prospecting and achieving your goals. See you in the next segment when we discover who your customer is.

What is an Ideal Customer Profile and a Buyer Persona

Who is your ideal customer? Customers must come first. Peter Drucker said the purpose of a business is to create and keep the customer to create or find the customer. Knowing who to target is our first step. Knowing who our customers are will make life and prosperity and sales a whole lot easier. Just look at how we can define who to target when we're prospecting. Well, we need to look at two aspects.

First of all, there is your ideal customer profile. And then we have a buyer persona. So what's the difference between a Nike customer profile and the buyer persona? When you understand who your customers are, you'd be able to adapt your prospecting methods to fit their needs, to be able to qualify new lives faster, you'll be able to modify your sales process to how they purchase and discover how your product or service satisfies their needs. So what's the difference between an ideal customer profile? And the buyer persona. So let's look at that. When would you use either one? Are there situations when your business could benefit from using both? Of them is an ideal customer profile. And then a customer profile is a profile of the perfect customer or business for your product or service. Who will benefit most from buying your service?

The ideal customer profile defines the characteristics of a company or a business that have the need for your product or services. By identifying what the common factors are in your top customers, you'll be able to better target the companies and businesses that are best suited for your product or services. In the next chapter, we will help you create an ideal customer profile in some depth, using an exercise to help you uncover your ideal customer. After you do the exercise in the next chapter, you will really know who your ideal customer is. You will know which businesses. You should be targeting your product or service.

What then is a buyer persona, a buyer persona is a semi fetish, no general representation of who the buyer is. Decision maker is within your ideal customer who will use buyer personas to focus on who you should be seeking out. What's your perspective? You're seeking them out in the business, people who have the authority and need to buy your product. The main difference between the ideal customer profile and buyer personas is that the ideal customer profile is based on statistical evidence from your CRM system, using analytical tools, gathering data from your existing customers.

The buyer persona that focuses on the individuals. Behind a purchase, the actual decision makers, the people who have the authority to buy your product or service. In the next two chapters, we'll help you define both your ideal customer profile and your buyer persona. So join us for these chapters to discover how you can find the people you need to Prospekt.

Creating an Ideal Customer Profile

Creating an ideal customer profile, an ideal customer profile is a description of a customer that would benefit immensely from your offering and that you can provide with significant value an ideal customer profile as a description of the company, not the individual buyer or end user, but someone, a company that is a perfect fit for your product or service, creating an ideal customer profile for your business as a tried and tested technique of generating more leads. An ideal customer profile is a hypothetical business or organization that would get the most value out of your product or service.

What is the ideal customer profile, as we discussed in our last chapter? An ideal customer profile is a profile or an example of the perfect customer or business for your product or service. The profile defines the characteristics of a company, our business that buys and values your product or services. By identifying what the common factors are and your top customers, you'll be able to better target the companies and businesses that are best suited for your product or services. And this venture will help you create an ideal customer profile in some depth, using an exercise and a template to help you uncover the characteristics of your ideal customer.

Your ideal customer is specific to your sales goals and to your product or service. It represents the type of business you want to focus on and acquire as a new customer with their business. The most important factor is ultimately that you will help the business improve their bottom line. You will also offer value and always like reducing their expenses and proving employees morale or elevating pinpoint solving problems and saving them time. Determining your ideal customer allows you to figure out which companies or businesses that you need to target when you're prospective.

The more detailed your profile is, the more accurately you'll be able to zone in on the companies that are most in need of your products or service and most likely to give you their businesses. The more specific your customer profile is, the more targeted your prospecting can be. Which means you'd be better able to identify and attract high quality leads who are ready to buy a detailed, high ideal customer profile will help you better understand how to reach out and sell to your customers, which means, Of course, more qualified leads, more appointments and ultimately more sales.

Let's look at how to create an ideal customer profile. Focus on the problem that your business is able to solve for your customers. And identify the type of businesses who face these challenges. Understand who your customers are and how they are using your product or service. And why are they using your product or service? And ideal customer customers, a business who is ready, willing and able to purchase your solution. Your profile should focus on relevant characteristics of your target accounts such as industry employee headcount and annual revenue, budget, geography, the technology that they're using, the size of their customer base and the level of their organizational management structure. To find your ideal customer, start by naming five companies who you have been successful with. What do they have in common? In which industry or industries do these companies work?

What is the size of these companies, revenue employees, or are they located? What are the biggest challenges they face? These are just some of the questions you might like to ask. Also include the questions of how big is the organization because of their revenue, customers, and employees. What job titles might be relevant? Which industry sector or niche is the organization and how long has the organization been in business? Where are they located? One of their pain points and goals? What does that mean? What problems can you solve for these companies? What value can you bring to these companies? What would stop them from choosing your offering? What is the one thing that makes your offer? The one they would choose.

Was the decision making process like what seasonal factors might play a part in the decision making? Which social media platforms do they use? What is the culture of the company? What are their values? With your ideal customer profile. At the ready, you can create a short list of companies to focus on and to prospect. An ideal customer profile delivers value to your business and prospective. It will help keep you more focused so that you spend your time concentrating on those customers who are most likely to by securing high quality leads, qualified prospects in our next venture will help you create a buyer persona and discover a fictitious representation of who the decision makers are within your ideal customer.

Creating a Buyer Persona

My persona focuses on the individuals behind the purchase, the actual decision makers, the people who have the authority to buy your product or service in this chapter. We will help you to find your buyer persona. A buyer persona is a semi fictional representation of your ideal buyer based on data interviews and perhaps some educated guesses. It is essentially a definition of your ideal via presented in a way that sounds like it is talking about a specific person. This is not a real customer, but a fictitious person who embodies the characteristics of your best potential customers.

Create your buyer persona to better understand who you can target on a deeper level and insure everyone you know how to. Support that target and work with these customers. This will help improve your reach and that will boost conversion rates and increase your prospecting activity. Give them. Buyer persona on the. Of course, you want those demographic details and centrist behavioral traits completed by a persona that may look like this. You will see your wish to discover his background. The demographics, his goals, the challenges he faces, common objections he may have to offer. His biggest fear. And his hobbies and interests.

Consider your feedback on the leads you have been interacting with the most. What generalizations can you make about the different types of decision makers you encounter, but prospective? Your existing customer base is the perfect place to start to discover your buyer persona. Because they've already purchased your product and service with your company. More precisely. Buyer persona may look like this. Once you have identified your ideal buyer persona, begin the information gathering process. By the following means, find answers to the following questions on Sobieraj role in the company. What type of company does he work for, and a level of education has the buyer achieved?

What's a binary gender? What is the buyer's age as a buyer in an urban, suburban or rural environment? How does the buyer spend his or her time? Hi tech savvy is the buyer. What social networks does the buyer prefer? One of the biggest challenges at work. How does the buyer define success in the workplace? What are the buyer's challenges? What are his career goals? One of the buyer's biggest fears. What is the buyer's age? And one of the most common concerns. How can you solve the buyer's challenges? How does the buyer prefer to make a buying decision, as they prefer to communicate with Kimie? A tablet can be found in the resources.

I would like you to complete your buyer persona, which contains these questions by following these steps and taking the time to correct these three key buyer personas for your company. You'll be more able to focus and target your prospects on social media. And in the next segment, we will show you where to find your ideal prospect. So don't forget to complete your buyer persona, and I will see you on where to find your prospect.

Summary

And summarize our last three chapters. First of all, we discussed an ideal customer profile, which is a description of a company or business that could benefit from your product or services, a company or a business that you can offer significant value. And I think a customer profile is a description of the company, not the individual prior or end user, a company that is a perfect fit for your product or service, creating an ideal customer profile. It's a tried and trusted technique for generating more leads, which will help you prospect more effectively and define the characteristics of the company.

Our business. On the other hand, the buyer persona focuses on the individuals behind the purchase, the actual decision makers and people who have the authority to buy your product or service, a buyer persona is a semi fetish, no representation of your ideal buyer based on interviews and some educated guesses.

It is essentially a definition of your ideal buyer presented in a way that sounds like it's talking about a specific person by creating a buyer persona. This will help you discover who to target when prospecting. Plus you'll be able to easily target potential customers on social media. In the next segment, we will show you how to research and find your ideal prospect.

Introduction to Prospecting with Social Media

Finding qualified prospects on social media. Social media prosperity is a free and easy way to connect with potential prospects that your business can help. Where can you find your potential customers, clients and businesses? Hopefully by now you've identified your ideal customer and both a buyer persona, so you know who you're seeking to develop as potential customers, as qualified leads if you have not completed your ideal customer profile or your buyer persona could encourage, you know, to go and download the worksheets. Having done this, you'll be able to identify those businesses and decision makers you need to focus on using social media.

The Internet provides unique opportunities to find potential customers and qualified leads. Build your relationships with them on social media. It's an easy way to build closer relationships. It's a networking tool using social media to generate leads. It's extremely effective when done right. When you're engaged in the business of prospecting, you need to take advantage of the information your potential clients and our customers provide. Online social media can provide you with several distinct advantages when used properly, such as reduced contact time.

Social media prospecting will reduce the time spent on searching for new potential prospects. A definite increase in the volume of leads is another advantage of using social media. You'll be able to discover better qualified prospects who can make buying decisions and provide you with the opportunity to build deeper relationships as well as helping you to achieve a shorter sales cycle. Ultimately, social selling is about building relationships. So let's look at what we can do in the next three chapters. We will focus on the Big Three social media networks for prosperity and demonstrate how you can succeed on each of these social platforms.

The Big Three are LinkedIn, Facebook and Twitter. And as you progress through the chapter, you will find a chapter on each of the Big Three, starting with LinkedIn. According to LinkedIn research, 50 percent of LinkedIn members are more likely to purchase from a company they engage with on LinkedIn. And the chapter link, then you will discover how to engage with prospects that facility then will focus on Facebook, what you will learn, how to engage actively with prospects and discover how you can trigger worthwhile conversations with Facebook Messenger next year by using Twitter to listen to and learn about your potential customers.

You may never have the cold call again. Discover how millions of business people turn to Twitter to connect to their interests, to share information and find out what's happening in the world. Learn how you can turn this to your advantage, all in the last chapter on Twitter. We were writing up the chapters in this chapter where we are focusing on prospecting the social media. And in the last chapter, we will look at YouTube, Instagram and Pinterest and see how you can use these social media platforms to enhance your prospects. So let's get started. And in the next year, discover the power of LinkedIn.

Prospecting on LinkedIn Part One

Why do people rob banks? It's because that's where the money is and LinkedIn is where the prospects are. So it makes good sense to be on LinkedIn and use it effectively to help you open the door to more prospects. I think of it as a business networking platform. Prospect on LinkedIn is an effective tool that drives 80 percent of business to business social media. A recent study by Weber Shandwick shows that LinkedIn is the preferred social network by CEOs. Visibility is important.

Engagement with your network of connections is the secret of success on LinkedIn. With a unique credibility, your profile needs to display you as a credible person. For success on LinkedIn, be sure to complete your profile and keep your profile up to date. A LinkedIn profile will help you become visible and the start of becoming noticed, getting noticed on LinkedIn, an updated profile is a great way to ensure that you can be found by the right person at the right time. 50 percent of your network success lies in presenting a complete, authentic profile and demonstrating your humanness. Here is a screen capture of my all star LinkedIn profile.

This is my professional profile on LinkedIn, just to give you an idea of what you need to aim for and what you need to create with your profile, with a banner at the top demonstrating what you do below that professional photograph and your name and qualifications. And then a couple of lines saying, what did you actually do? Moving on, don't tell you more about what you do I and my role helping CEOs than I have chapters, some chapters I've created, loaded up to my LinkedIn profile. But you need to do this on my dashboard, which tells me my views, both views and how many people have been searching for me and my recent activity. It shows you how many followers I have. And then my job, my experience and my present job is excellent. You want to put your job there.

Describe for me what you actually do in the job and the previous jobs, my skill and then my qualifications. Some of the examples that I have, some of the diplomas that I hold and that shows you the volunteer experience, where do you volunteer and even fill that up? You can add new skills and people will endorse you on your skills who know you. Then they will give you a recommendation. Some people who know me that I've worked with and spoken with and given me recommendations of what they feel, how I perform in my role. So I want to ask people for recommendations. And below that, Books, organizations, publications, some people I follow on LinkedIn. So although you can create a personal profile, mine is an All-Star profile. And how do you get an all star profile?

You fill out completely each part of that profile and tell the people about your profile will improve your chances of being visible and signed on search engines in addition to building your personal profile on LinkedIn. Does the company have a business page, a business page may look like this. This is my company's business page. Let's have a look at the sales excellence business page and see what you need to create your own company page. This is my company's page, sales excellence. You see, you have the banner at the top. Plus, I have posted some chapters, some content on it, which may be of interest to my followers. You'll see that I can check what the process is on the page.

You can see that my main visitors are business development people, sales people. So those are the type of people I want to attract to my page. So get my page up, send company information out, and get my company website.

And that can see from my visitor analytical that we had 50 odd views of the page so far in the last period. The chapters attract people to the page and see what we are doing, presenting various projects and content that will be of interest to the people. So one of the things you need to do is think about content that you can put on your company page that will help your prospects, find out who you are and what you do so all your employees can be on this one page that you have a career. Once you have built your personal profile and perhaps a business page, you can start to build your network of connections on LinkedIn.

You can begin building your professional networking by connecting with professional contacts that you know and trust within your network is a great way to stay in touch with colleagues, customers and clients, as well as connecting with new professional opportunities, which we will talk about in the next chapter. Start by inviting people you know and trust and be one of the first three degree connections who are given access to any information that you have on your profile on LinkedIn to grow your network search or email, search or email address, book to find contacts and invite them to connect with you on LinkedIn using their email address.

With these connections, you will be able to see who they are connected with to those second degree connections and you will be able to connect with them. I would advise you not to make any connections ad hoc think. Why would you want to make this connection? Have you built your network of personal contacts? You can now move to building connections with prospects that you want to do business with. Next year you will find and discover how to connect with prospects on LinkedIn.

Prospecting on LinkedIn Part Two

Both your buyer persona and I do customer profile, you already know who your ideal target is. And to convert this into LinkedIn Prospect's focus on these questions, in which sector does my ideal customer work in? What city region does he live in? Does he work locally, nationally, internationally? What is his job title and what is his seniority level? Is he a first or second level connection on LinkedIn? From your persona and idea of customer profile, you're ready to apply the strategy to discover potential prospects and customers.

And the last one actually spoke about the credibility factor of your LinkedIn profile when your potential customer visits your personal profile. Is it well presented and professional? Does it tell the story? Explaining who you are, what you do and how you do all this increases your chances of getting your connection request accepted. I see how you can use your ideal customer profile to help you identify possible prospects on LinkedIn. A search bar can be seen at the top of any LinkedIn page you're reviewing allows you to search for people, companies, locations and more than just demonstrate how you can use the search facility on LinkedIn using the keywords in your ideal customer profile into the search bar of the top of the page, then you can select an option from the suggestions you'll be directed to your selection.

You will see more results by clicking the search icon to run the search. See your results at the bottom of the dropdown. You'll be redirected to the search results page. Or you can sneak by people, jobs, events, content companies, schools, groups, etc. there you can find to your search. You can also add some additional search variables to narrow down your search results. Assuming you're using search to grow your network, you first may want to check out the second option under

Connexions. So you're only getting results from people you're not connected to, but you can both be connected to someone in common and think about the job title or keywords that someone would have in his profile that you'd like to connect with.

Click on the keywords option to reveal more additional choices, the title company, school, etc. Let's look at this example. How you can search on LinkedIn. We find our search bar at the top. Let's say we're looking for CEOs and through that and then we get the drop down menu. You can see all these people are looking for different people and you'll see names coming up of all people with the title of CEO. And what we want to do is look at our connections. We'll find their first and second connections. So we click first and second connections because we'll be able to connect directly with those people, and will be able to send them a message that we want to go to locations. So do we want locally, nationally or internationally?

We get to choose locations here. So choose your locations and then put that filter in and that will refine your search even more and you can create a search alert. And that's where all filters up open to the right, as you can see. Now, as we scroll down to the right, you can refine their search. Let's say you want to find people in information technology and people in computer software. So type that into the box and then have to turn again. And you'll see that we get a new refined list of the people. So then we can decide who we are going to connect with. So we choose this one that looks like a likely prospect. And we want to add the note. So we click on a note.

We can send a message asking them to connect and we'll show you in a moment. We will talk about your message in a moment. But first, let's look at LinkedIn, LinkedIn allows you to connect one to one with nearly anyone in the world. Don't squander this opportunity by sending a sales pitch. It's unprofessional and likely to get a response.

Connecting on LinkedIn is like going on a blind date. You would not ask someone to marry you on the first date, would you? You would build the relationship first. Your objective on LinkedIn is to build a relationship and to nurture the relationship. And we will talk about nurturing lead liver in this Book.

By crafting that personalized note, you're more likely to get connected. Please remember your objective is not, I repeat, I repeat, not to sell online LinkedIn. Your objective is to build a relationship and take the conversation offline, as you would at a networking event. The objective is to introduce yourself when you see someone you do not know well but you're hoping to speak with. You usually give him or her a one sentence background. Hi, I'm calling. I see we have a couple of connections in common and I would like to connect thanks in advance or I'm calling and I loved your latest blog post content or whatever they have written about and I would like to connect thanks in advance. You may also want to include your mutual contact or your shared background TV. Your introduction for the specific contact shows that you're serious about connecting with Hamaha. You'll find an example of introduction messages that you can tailor for your own use in the resources as you build the relationship.

Ask yourself why you want to be connected. Do you like this person as our product? Do you want to ask this person questions about his or her background? Follow his posts on LinkedIn, look at his or her company website, and you're looking for an opportunity to have a professional discussion of interest to them. Make sure you ask appropriately and correspond with appropriate connections to your relationship, and as you move the relationship forward and start to have a rapport with your connection, share information which may be of value to them. And when the time is right, you should ask for permission to email them, or you may send a chapter introduction. Remember, your goal is to develop your relationship to a point where you can take the conversation offline.

Prospecting on Facebook

Facebook is no longer just for finding old classmates, looking at cookie cooking chapters are very year kittens. You can tell by their relationships with the contacts you have already made on LinkedIn in the previous chapter. This way, you can develop a more intimate relationship with your LinkedIn contacts. You will discover more of our lifestyle and find common interests to build your relationship with. You're trying to connect with real people. They will hopefully become your prospects and customers treat them like real people and they will do the same for you.

Use Facebook as a touch point because Facebook's search is less powerful than LinkedIn. Consider using Facebook to build rapport with the buyer after you have identified them as a potential fit for you. Not only does this keep you in front of their mind, but your prospect is also likely to accept your request because you are familiar. Remember to be human for your social media perspective to be effective. You want to be crystal clear about what you want to achieve. Ask yourself what is your goal? What message do you want to deliver? Thanks to your prospects profile, you have access to a ton of information, usually details to build rapport. For example, If you both like a certain film, for example. That's you, Starwars, you might start a conversation by saying something like hi from a fellow Star Wars fan.

I'm wondering if I should open the conversation. He will know who you are targeting from your buyer persona, discover your prospects, hobbies and interests, you can also take advantage of their work history. Many people fill out their Facebook profiles with their current and former job titles and employers. Once you discover who you want to connect with, do not. And I repeat again, do not send a friend request right away. Don't send a friend request right away. Follow your prospect initially and like their posts and follow this up by making valuable comments on their posts almost. Look where you can add value to your prospects. Then I have to connect, as you will have become both visible and familiar to them by liking their posts like in their comments and following them on Facebook.

You'll also need to build what is called a Facebook fan page or business page. A Facebook fan page is a business account that represents a company or organization that looks similar to a Facebook profile. Creating a Facebook fan page allows the more than two billion people that are on Facebook to discover you and your business. Think of your page as a digital shopfront. Setting up a business page is simple and free. And it looks great on both desktop and mobile. It offers unique tools for you to manage and track engagement. So take the opportunity to build your fanpage, you can use this to attract prospects, so. Here is how. So let me show you how you can build your fanpage, so building your fan page starts by putting your page name in here, let's call it a sales training company, and you'll see the name comes up above. Cavallari got to change your category and so you have to cut in there.

And that's Chew's, business consultant from the drop down menu. Then we got to add a description which began with Piast in Nemr ready to create our Arpège Fumie. Create a page that will allow us to add a profile picture so we choose a profile picture from which we can upload that. Then we choose a banner and click on the banner, drag the banner into place where we need it. So then you can see that you can add buttons, you can start selling from your page and you click get started. And that will then show that your page is ready and choose what you want to do with your page. You can also join groups on Facebook, which will help you to find more prospects to join the group, go to your profile page and from your profile page or from your news page, click groups in the left menu, in the search bar at the top. Enter some keywords for the group you're looking for. Select the group, then click.

Join the group below the cover photo. Select where you like to join as your profile or your page and click join group. Depending on the group settings, you may have to wait for a group admin to approve your request using keywords from your customer. Ideal profile. Here's an example of how you can find prospects to link to on Facebook groups.

We will discuss in a later chapter how you can add content both here and on LinkedIn. Content will help you to attract more prospects both on Facebook and LinkedIn. Facebook is not a shotgun approach. It's a one to one communication. To start communicating with your prospects using Facebook Messenger, then you are starting to move the relationship forward using Facebook Messenger to build the relationship. And as we spoke about in our last chapter on LinkedIn, the goal is to take the conversation offline, share information of interest to your prospect, and open a conversation about the information. What are their thoughts on it? People aren't messaging. More and more people crave human connections. And with messaging, making connections is easier than ever.

It is perhaps no surprise that messaging has become an integral part of people's daily lives. If you're ever if you've ever messaged someone to ask if it's a good time to give them a call, then you are aware that you've already used an experience. This new method of contact. Facebook Messenger also allows you to make a fist of this phone call. Always ask permission before making your call with Facebook Messenger. You can take the message offline, which is your goal, as we discussed in LinkedIn. So on all social media, your goal is to have an offline conversation. In our next chapter, we will show you three more methods of getting prospects. They are Twitter, Instagram and YouTube.

Prospecting on Twitter

Finding prospects on Twitter is all about who you follow and who follows you with more than 300 million people to choose from. It will take a bit of effort to find your target audience. Start by identifying and searching for keywords and hashtags your potential buyers might use using the Twitter search, then follow anyone who matches your ideal customer profile. Also, search for your LinkedIn and Facebook connections.

Know that you've built up your following list. It's time to start listening by monitoring your feed to find those you're most able to help and who are most open to your product or service. Search for terms like Can anyone recommend or can anyone give us advice on how to identify those looking for immediate assistance? Keep an eye on it for buying signals, dissatisfaction with a competitor or exhibiting a need. Your product or service can fulfill and engage at the beginning of the sales cycle. Or if you can stop the buying process or imminent sale, jump in and get on the shortlist. You can combine a very precise Twitter search with a service called And let me spell it for you. A particularly interesting tweet appears Twitter is the perfect research tool for prospective research. You can use it to keep an eye on the company outlook of your contact. You can follow those to get a better sense of their challenges, goals and agendas.

For example, even if your sales contact is the head of networking who you may wish to contact, you can find out a huge amount about their company from a head of product by building the list of people you follow. You also need to build up your own following to build up your own following. You need a clear and focused value that explains exactly what you and your company does. A good value show in your areas of expertise will make people much more likely to follow you back. The best thing about Twitter is that it's easy to strike up a conversation with your target audience, but to avoid coming off like this. It's crucial you start by showing them you're listening. Your goal, as always, is to take the conversation offline.

The aim is for your Twitter feed to become a source of great content and thought provoking comments that are relevant to the audience you want to attract when sharing links. Use link shorteners like pettily. Not only will it free up more characters for your tweet, it also allows you to track clicks, shares and shares. So you're sure you can engage with anyone who's shown interest in your links, create a list of your prospects so you can easily interact with them. Look for what they're tweeting about. Are they pushing out their own blogs? If you read, tweet them and add a comment of your own.

As you read tweets, you will get more interaction. Also, be sure to send them content that is relevant and useful to them. You can also use the list to get valuable information about your prospects. And the idea is that you can further your relationship with those prospects. Also, follow your competitors, see what they're up to. The essence of Twitter is listening and retweeting good content. Remember, the goal is to build a relationship and take the conversation offline.

Prospecting on Instagram

Most social marketers don't think of Instagram as a lead generating platform, but they're missing out. Here's how to get more leads on Instagram. Roughly 80 percent of crimes follow the business on Instagram, which is already a pretty good sign of intent that marketers can tap into. Even better, 80 percent of Facebook's survey respondents say they use Instagram to decide whether or not to buy something. If you're not collecting leads on Instagram, you're missing out.

Did you know that Instagram's number of active monthly users are growing at a faster rate than Facebook, Twitter and Snapchat? So you need help to get in on the action and walk you through degenerate leads on Instagram with proven tips in 2015. Instagram reached an astonishing one billion active monthly users, as well as at least 25 million business profiles worldwide. So we need to create an Instagram business profile quickly in this kind of not difficult procedure, as you must have gone through this before and stolen the app and made an account. And one of two ways you can sign up is by using your email address or even your contact number and entering the user name and the cash. You already have a Facebook account.

You can login with the same account details and link them together. You can now connect to your Facebook business page to establish online contacts. You can get the benefit of work that you have done from the settings menu. You can choose the Invite Facebook friends option to send a notification to the whole network of Facebook to access other networks. You can use the option. Invite friends such as LinkedIn, Gmail or Yahoo! Contact. One of the easiest ways to step up engagement is simply to respond to everything except the spam, Of course, but don't use it throughout the account. Thanks.

And carry on with your day if you really want to grow your audience and Instagram needs, you have to take some time to dig a bit deeper and craft a thoughtful response. Come up with interesting and visually appealing ways to show off the best bits of your brand, industry and products if you're unsure what types of things you should focus on. Check out what other companies in your industry do and find out and see what they're doing or even go outside of your industry to other companies for inspiration. You should be posting a regular Instagram post at least once a day. And there are tools like Buffer, HootSuite, all those are available to help you scale your posts in advance and keep you on track. And finally check your Instagram and articles to access analytics and Instagram. See here, if you already have an Instagram business, our Twitter profile, you can easily access your analytics through the insights tab and the Instagram.

I'll start by tapping on the menu icon and the top right corner of your profile. Then click on the Insights tab, which will open the analytics for your business or create our profile. Once you open your insights, you'll be able to find a ton of metrics and articles for your post. Instagram can show you under the vehicles for post stories that you published after you've switched to a business, our creator profile, Instagram Analytical Features gives you a visual overview of how your posts and stories are performing. Download the app from the App Store, then sign up and you can sign up using your Facebook login.

Prospecting on YouTube

In the early stages of the buyer's journey, customers are prospects trying to find out as much about how to solve their business problems, and they're looking for potential solutions. This not only leads them to sites like YouTube, where they may end up watching multiple company or product chapters. One of your main priorities as a prospector is to build awareness of your business and start a long term relationship with your potential customers.

As many people don't realize, your issue is an effective way to rank higher in our organic search. If you craft a good description under the chapter, that will help you with your SEO. YouTube is the second largest search engine in the world and gets over 30 million visitors every single day. And because 70 percent of buyers turn to Google search to do this, there's a massive potential for companies to leverage YouTube CEO to rank in both Google and YouTube.

The first step is obviously not producing a chapter that ranks high in your niche is finding the right keywords. You should find keywords that have your YouTube chapter results on the first page of Google so that your chapter also has a high likelihood of ranking near the top of the page, the relevant search terms. For example, this YouTube chapter appears on the first page of Google, but the phrase ten mistakes on the telephone. Keeping your chapter title at least five words long allows you to include your full keyword. The keyword stuffing you tube gives you a slight boost if you put your keyword at the beginning of your title, right, a high quality description of your YouTube chapter description as how YouTube determines what the content of the chapter is about. This is one of the most important parts of uploading your chapter on YouTube.

By keeping these points in mind, you can skyrocket the reach of your chapter so that you rank high in both YouTube and Google searches, get the attention of more prospects and ultimately convert them into long term paying customers at a later chapter. We will discuss how to create chapters for prospective customers.

Sales Funnel and Customer Relationship Management

Having made your connections on social media, LinkedIn, Facebook, Twitter, Instagram and YouTube. How will you manage your prospective strategy? How will you ensure you follow up with prospects, open conversations and ensure everything is in the one place when prospecting for new business? The process is not a straight line. You need to be in control of that process. Converting a lead to a customer often takes its own Book and varies from business to business. Whether you're a B2B or B2C, it is important for you when prospecting to understand and envision your latest journey so that you can reach the goal of winning an appointment, having a system to manage your leads and follow a step by step process. And this will help you avoid prospecting in the dark. It's a series of steps that develop into what is called the cell phone.

To implement your sales funnel, you need a CRM system, a customer relationship management software. This will help you manage and measure your sales funnel and help improve the efficiency of your sales process to convert leads to customers. You may hear the term sales pipeline, but some people think it's the same as a sales phone. Sales funnel and sales pipeline are often misunderstood to do the same thing. The sales funnel and the sales pipeline are completely different, the sales funnel is about leads when you're prospecting. The sales pipeline is about deals, the sales funnel is the stages in the process your leads go through before coming.

Customers, warehouses, and sales pipeline comprises every stage in your sales process. Moving the sale from the start to the close to the sales funnel looked like yourself. I'll start with all your contact leads at the top of the funnel. Initially they are elite. Then you qualify the lead to become a prospect. You make contact, take the conversation offline and make an appointment. Yourself, I'll start with all your contact leads at the top of the funnel, initially they relate, then you qualify the lead to become a prospect. You make contact, take the conversation offline and make an appointment. Adopting a CRM system with sales funnel management capabilities, possible fate impacts on your prospects and performance. That's a look at how you can use a CRM system to feed and fill your sales, funnel a CRM tracks all your prospecting activities, which helps you to know when you need to follow up with specific prospects.

When you're reminded about specific follow ups, you schedule a point in time when it is most helpful to follow up with that prospect. This way you increase the chances of converting more of your leads into customers, and CRM will provide you with one place where you can keep track of leads, prospects and customers over any duration of time. CRM Also allows you to review specific activities like emails, calls and meetings. But using a CRM system will boost your productivity. Keeping all your information regarding prospects in a central location will help you close more sales and faster important business relationships. There are numerous CRM systems available.

According to Kept Teria, the top 10 CRM systems are Salesforce, HubSpot, CRM, Money.com, Cupper, Zen Tech Sell Active Campean, Fresh Works Type Drive, Really Simple Systems and Zoho my favorite, which I use as HubSpot, which is rated number two backup carrier HubSpot offers a free version which is perfect for prospected the free sales HubSpot offers like chat links to your emails, links to your calendar, email scheduling, email tracking and notifications, also email templates and meeting schedules and reporting dashboard where you can have a view of your sales funnel messenger integration. And HubSpot is available as a mobile app. That's how HubSpot works to start off with a screen like this.

Once you register your TV contacts and if you want to add a contact, create a contact that says that you're a Blackbelt gift card. Mike Rowe, self doubt. Come to your father, Bill, and you've got him on LinkedIn. His last name is Kit. His job title is not, say, CEO, phone number is plus one, that is a league. So you do that. He's a new league career contact and a major league player because Bill Gates, we got to sign Bill Gates this screen and I opened it up. I'm going to see that. I have updated it on the left. You'll see we've got Bill Gates, CEO and Microsoft. We can make notes. We can email people, we can make a telephone call, we can log a call, or we can set a task together, make a call, send an email or set up a meeting. All the details. But Bill, time the left hand side for the side. You will see we've got Microsoft.

If we preview that, it actually will give you and we'll give you all the details about the company, Microsoft Garmin phone number, tell you what the company does and what their address is, what type of a company linked to them on LinkedIn and all the information is there on HubSpot. So now you can create a task, let's say that you want to create a task set up to email battle or to set up a meeting with Bill Gates as your first lead. Then you have all your data in there and you can start working with them on HubSpot. With your CRM system in place, you can fill your sales funnel with prospects and you can proceed to contact your leads and start to message them to build a relationship and move the conversation forward. Our next chapter is on how to message prospects on social media so you can bring the conversation offline, which is your goal at this point.

How to Message on Social Media

He most probably would agree that sales conversations on social media can be tricky. Some salespeople simply lack the necessary skills, and are ready to go too far to sell a product or service when sending messages on social media. Statistics support this rate. Only 15 percent of sales people have trusted respected advisors. 66 percent of salespeople are regarded as just being average. Only 31 percent of B2B salespeople have effective conversations with prospects. This leaves a lot of room for improvement instead of blatantly pitching your offer. You need to make a radical shift and show that you genuinely care about your prospects.

There is no such thing as selling on social media, on LinkedIn, Facebook and all the other social media platforms. The objective is simply to build a relationship, a relationship that you can take the conversation offline or you can have that real sales conversation. The goal of a direct message, either to a new connection or our new connection on social media is to start a conversation and build a relationship. What you are seeking from your message is a reply, not a conversion to a CEO, your goal is to increase engagement with your leaders and hopefully you can qualify them and turn them into prospect's deciding who and how to send a message on LinkedIn or on Facebook, which you will use as a messenger.

Let's say that's a new connection. Thank them for connecting. Ask them if you can make any introductions to your connections, ask them who would be a good introduction for you. You're building a conversation. Then a follow up direct message asked how they would add value to your introductions and continue engaging and building rapport, we will discuss in a moment how to take that conversation offline. Next step is to look at who liked or made comments on your

LinkedIn or Facebook posts remembering you are building a relationship now. One of the first and best books I have read on selling was How to Win Friends and Influence People by a gentleman called Dale Carnegie. Gayle's book was published back in the 30s. But yet Carnegie's insights are as relevant today as back in the 30s, the essence of the book is six ways to make people like you.

No one becomes genuinely interested in all the people to smile, remember? And number three, remember that a person's name is to that person the sweetest and most important sign in any language. Number four, be a good listener. Number five, talk in terms of the other person's interests. At number six, making the other person feel important and doing it sincerely. Next, find out what groups on social media your lead is active in. Join them. And start posting and then getting on those groups again. Look who has left your post or made a comment on social media after someone has liked or commented on something you or someone else has said on social media. You can send a simple message, a message such as this. John, I see you like my comment on whatever the comment may relate to. Continue by saying thank you for the like.

Our comment, whatever the case may be. I see you, John, you certainly again, a mention of the role of John. I see that you're a business development manager with ABC Inc. I love to have a conversation with you sometime and sign it with just your first name. When responding to comments on social media, make sure you try to connect with each person. Use the first name and personalize your response so they do not feel that you're just entertaining them. Remember, people do business with those they know, like trust and respect, and if they reply now, you have started to engage with them. And remember number five and six from Dale Carnegie, talk in terms of their interests and make them feel important. And, Of course, dear, sincerely. I'll also follow the four touch points rule.

What are the forward touch touchpoint rules? Well, a common mistake I see business owners make when sending LinkedIn prospective messages is giving up after not receiving a response after their first or second message. Have you heard of the Ford Touch Point Road until you receive a reply from a prospect you should make for touch point, that is, send a Ford message over a period of one to two months if you do not receive a response from your first one. Send another message in one to two weeks. Try to approach this message from another angle, if you do not receive a response, send another message after one or two weeks and then again about one month later, send one final message after your previous messages.

When they do reply, have a conversation with them about their role or challenges and goals. Then when you have both the conversation to a place that you're ready to go offline, the most effective way to take that offline is within the invite chapter that has proved to have a 60 to 70 percent response rate compared to only a five response rate with e-mail. I will be discussing emails later. He is 82 years old. I personally use that yard. There's a free version and there are others available, Of course. It is an app for your smartphone and you can provide a link to your calendar using calendar. Here's a sample chapter I made on my iPhone for John Smith. We're friends on LinkedIn. We have spoken a few times there. I'd like to have a conversation with you offline and we'll send you my calendar and we can make a couple of times when it suits you to talk. See how simple it is to make a chapter. You can start sending messages on your social media right now and take that conversation offline.

Conclusion

Finding qualified prospects in social media is a free and easy way to connect with potential customers. In this series of chapters, you discovered your potential customers, clients and businesses using social media. You're introduced to the Big Three social media platforms LinkedIn, Facebook and Twitter.

Also, we looked at YouTube and Instagram and discovered how you can find leads and prospects on these platforms. We discussed how to set up a series of highly qualified leads to become prospects. There's no such thing as social solidarity. Social media are the platforms where you build relationships. You'll have learned how to properly message prospects and take the conversation offline.

Don't miss out!

Visit the website below and you can sign up to receive emails whenever SADANAND PUJARI publishes a new book. There's no charge and no obligation.

https://books2read.com/r/B-A-YJFBB-KMARC

BOOKS 2 READ

Connecting independent readers to independent writers.

Also by SADANAND PUJARI

Master The Psychology Of Weight Loss Via Hypnosis Build Healthy Sleep Habits Learn The Art Of Meditation
Improve People Management And Build Employee Engagement

Milton Keynes UK
Ingram Content Group UK Ltd.
UKHW022005011223
433620UK00014B/790